Trevor Po

The Mental Health Handbook
Revised Edition

Speechmark Publishing Ltd
Telford Road, Bicester, Oxon OX26 4LQ, UK

To David, Tanya, Jonathan, Sarah and Hannah

Trevor Powell BA (Hons), PsychD, AFBPs, C Psychol is an experienced practising Consultant Clinical Psychologist who has worked in the field of Adult Mental Health within the Health Service for the last twenty years. As a therapist he works with clients both individually and in groups, running group training courses such as Anxiety Management and Assertiveness Training. He has carried out and published research on short-term therapy with individuals and groups, and has experience of running local and national workshops for other health care professionals. Trevor is the co-author of *Anxiety and Stress Management* (Routledge, 1990), and the author of *Head Injury: A Practical Guide* (Winslow, 1994) and *Stress-Free Living* (Dorling Kindersley, 1997). He is married with children, and lives in Berkshire.

Published by
Speechmark Publishing Ltd, Telford Road, Bicester, Oxon OX26 4LQ, United Kingdom
www.speechmark.net

First published in 1992
Second Edition 2000, 2001

002-4626/Printed in the United Kingdom/1010

British Library Cataloguing in Publication Data
Powell, Trevor J., 1955–
   The mental health handbook. – Rev. ed.
   1. Mental health   2. Mentally ill – Rehabilitation
   I. Title
   362.2

ISBN 0 86388 330 3
(previously published by Winslow Press Ltd under ISBN 0 86388 256 0)

Contents

Introduction to the First Edition

I would like to begin by acknowledging my debt to all those people whose thoughts, ideas, theories and writings have made this book possible. Throughout this handbook, I have tried to reference the original source of material, but this has not always been possible. It seems to me that most ideas and writings are developments, enlargements and elaborations of other people's work and that this is especially true in the field of mental health. I will take this opportunity firstly to apologise to any who may feel that their ideas are being reprinted as my own and secondly to claim little originality for these pages.

The idea of bringing together this conglomeration of material in handout form stems from a number of sources. First, in the clinical psychology department where I work there are two old filing cabinets full of rather tatty, poorly printed handouts. Some of these have been written by members of the department, others have been brought in by trainees on placement, whilst others have been borrowed or copied from other people. These handouts have been very popular and in constant demand. For a number of years I have been meaning to rewrite and retype them; that wish has now been fulfilled in this collection. Second, I strongly believe that printed handouts can have a very useful role to play in some types of therapeutic intervention. I remember one occasion when an anxious client informed me that she always carried my handouts around in her handbag and, if she was feeling anxious on the bus, she would read them and feel reassured. We all forget things, particularly when we are feeling upset, and having material assistance in the form of these handouts can be of great help to many people. Third, cognitive behavioural psychotherapy is largely about challenging and changing people's thinking, as a way of helping them changing their behaviour and the way that they feel. To do that effectively, focused, relevant, written information is very important. These handouts are the result of an amalgamation and condensation of a wide range of material, presented as concise single page documents.

The handouts should be used as an aid to a therapeutic intervention, not as a substitute. They should be used as tools. When you buy a tool box, you do not expect to find instructions on how to use a chisel or a wood plane. Similarly, in the case of this 'tool box' there are no written instructions. You select the appropriate 'tool' and apply it as you see fit. References are provided if you or your client need further information.

Finally, each handout is designed to be photocopied for therapeutic use. Some of the handouts comprise more than one sheet and can be stapled together. I hope that you find this a useful resource.

Trevor Powell

Consultant Clinical Psychologist
West Berkshire Health Authority
June 1992

Introduction to the Revised Edition

I am very pleased that the *Mental Health Handbook* has been so popular over the last eight years and indeed I still use it myself. However, since its first publication our knowledge of treatment strategies for mental health problems has increased substantially and so it is time for a second edition. Although the revised edition has a new design and layout, the basic characteristics of offering photocopiable handouts is still the same. The main theoretical underpinning of the book is still predominantly cognitive behavioural therapy, which offers an educational, instructive and directive approach to solving specified problems. The handouts are an aid to therapeutic intervention and not a substitute.

I have updated existing pages and added some new ones. There are new pages in the first section on Social Phobia, Somatic Anxiety, Coping with Worry and Trauma. The section on Assertiveness has added pages on Overcoming Sulking. In the third section on Depression there are new pages on Bereavement and improving Self-Care. The section on Stress has new pages on Procrastination. Within the Disorders of Habit section there are new pages on various aspects of Health Psychology, which has blossomed over the last decade, including expanded Pain Management, Chronic Fatigue, Headaches, Irritable Bowel Syndrome, an extended section on Anger Management and extended pages on Relationship Enhancement. In the final section, which deals more with chronic mental illnesses, is an improved section on Coping and Managing the Symptoms of Schizophrenia, including a new self-monitoring questionnaire.

I hope that this second, revised edition is as useful and as popular as the first edition. I would like to reiterate that the ideas in this book do not belong to me, but, I hope, reflect our common pool of knowledge. So, if readers have any new ideas or information that would enhance the quality of the book, they would be received with gratitude.

Trevor Powell

Consultant Clinical Psychologist
May 2000

Acknowledgements

Firstly, thanks to my wife, Meriel, for her love and support, encouragement and patience. Secondly, thanks to Liz, and all those at CST in Reading, who typed and retyped the document and never once made me feel a nuisance. Thirdly, thanks to Alistair Keddie, Head of the Clinical Psychology Department, West Berkshire Health Authority, who made this project possible.

I would also like to thank to a number of authors who gave permission to publish specific material: Professor Isaac Marks for permission to publish the Fear Questionnaire; Dr Snaith for permission to publish the Hospital Anxiety and Depression Scale; Dr Bob Wycherly for permission to publish his diagram on Irrational Thinking habits; and Professor Cary Cooper for help on the work stress questionnaire. Lastly, I would like to thank all those others, authors, therapists and clinicians whose work has made this book possible.

Acknowledgements (Second Edition)

I would like to thank all my colleagues who have made contributions to this edition especially Dr Mary Whalley, Alistair Keddie, Sue Cummings, Dr Margaret Roberts and Dr Jo Smith for the use of the Early Signs Scale.

SECTION 1 – MANAGING ANXIETY

MANAGING ANXIETY

▪ Books for Professionals

Andrews S G, Crino R, Hunt C, Lampe L & Page A, *Treatment of Anxiety Disorders,* Cambridge University Press, 1994.

Beck A T, Emery G & Greenberg R, *Anxiety Disorders and Phobias: A Cognitive Perspective,* Basic Books, New York, 1985.

Hawton K, Salkovskis P, Kirk J & Clark D, *Cognitive Behaviour Therapy for Psychiatric Problems,* Oxford University Press, Oxford, 1989.

Kowalski R, *Anxiety & Stress Management Toolkit,* Winslow Press, Bicester, 1999.

Wells A, *Cognitive Therapy of Anxiety Disorders,* Wiley, London, 1998.

▪ Books for Clients

Bailey R, *Systematic Relaxation Pack,* Winslow Press, Bicester, 1990.

Bourne EJ, *The Anxiety and Phobia Workbook,* New Harbinger, Oakland, CA, 1990.

Butler G, *Overcoming Social Anxiety and Shyness,* Robinson Publishing Ltd, 1999.

De Silva P & Rachman S, *Obsessive-Compulsive Disorder: The Facts,* Oxford University Press, Oxford, 1992.

Ingram C, *Panic Attacks: what they are, why they happen and what you can do about them,* London, Thorson, 1993.

Madders J, *Stress and Relaxation,* Martin Dunitz, Cambridge, 1979.

Marks I M, *Living with Fear,* McGraw Hill, New York, 1978.

Powell T J, *Stress Free Living,* Dorling Kindersley, 2000.

Weeks C, *Self-Help for Your Nerves,* Angus and Robertson, London, 1962.

▪ Addresses

MIND (National Association for Mental Health), Granter House, 15–19 Broadway, London E15 4BY.
Tel 020 8522 1728 and 08457 660163.

The National Phobics Society, Zion Centre, Royce Road, Hulme, Manchester M15 5FQ.
Tel 0161 227 9898.

Fear of Flying Courses. Information from British Airways Customer Relations at Heathrow Airport or direct from Avia Tours. Tel 01252 793250 or 0161 832 7972

References

'Nothing in life is to be feared it is only to be understood'

– Madame Curie –

◼ Types of anxiety problem

Tension and anxiety are common problems. About one tenth of the population every year will see their doctor because they feel tense or anxious. In the past doctors have traditionally prescribed drugs for such problems, but over the last few years research has shown that there are more effective ways of treating anxiety. This new approach involves teaching people how to cope, and these methods are similar to learning a new skill such as riding a bicycle or learning to play the piano.

These approaches can help a variety of people whose problems on the surface may take a different form, but who underneath suffer the same unpleasant feelings. Examples include the housebound person who is terrified of going out; the person who is afraid of spiders, lifts, aeroplanes, or small spaces (these problems are called phobias); the person who experiences panic attacks; the person who obsessively checks things such as all the electrical appliances or compulsively washes their hands. Lastly, there may be people who feel generally anxious and who cannot tie their feelings down to anything specific.

◼ Anxiety is a normal reaction

Anxiety is a normal healthy reaction. It happens to everyone at times of danger or in worrying situations. There is a perception of threat or danger to either your physical or psychological well being. When you are anxious your bodily system speeds up. In certain circumstances this can be a definite advantage. It means that your are ready for action and enables you to respond quickly if necessary. Moderate amounts of anxiety actually improve your performance, spurring you on to greater achievements.

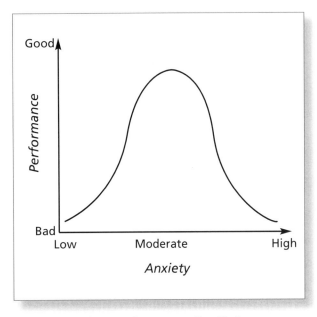

The graph above – known as the Yerkes-Dodson curve – demonstrates this point. People were given a task which involved remembering some numbers. But as they did this they were made anxious, some a little, some a lot, some in between. As the graph shows, when the anxiety was low or high the people did not perform well, but when their anxiety was moderate they did best.

Anxiety becomes a problem when it interferes with our performance or our everyday lives. This is when it becomes necessary to learn how to control it. Remember that anxiety is a normal healthy reaction. You cannot banish it completely from your life but you can learn to manage it.

■ Anxiety and your body

When we feel anxious a chain of automatic events occurs in our bodies, which prepares us for action. This reaction is often termed the 'fight or flight' response and can be traced back into our evolutionary past. Imagine the primitive caveman threatened by a wild animal. He needs to be prepared for vigorous action: either to run or to fight. We still possess this survival reaction, although it is now triggered by more subtle situations – some of which we are not even consciously aware of.

The reaction itself consists of the brain sending a message to pump adrenalin into the bloodstream and into the large skeletal muscles of the arms and legs. The heart beats faster as it is working harder. Because it is working harder, it needs more fuel so we breathe in more oxygen. To cool down the body, sweat and blood capillaries come to the surface. The body ideally needs to be as light as possible so a visit to the toilet might be necessary. When this chain of events occurs in a normal situation, for example if we are pushing a trolley around a supermarket or sitting in a business meeting, it can be very frightening. The important thing to remember is that the physical symptoms are natural and not harmful, but are appearing in an inappropriate situation.

■ The three systems of anxiety

Anxiety is often referred to as if it is a single phenomenon, but this is not the case. There are three parts to the feeling of anxiety:

❶ **Bodily sensations:** These have already been mentioned – they include irregular breathing, churning stomach, sweating, trembling, racing heart and the need to visit the toilet.

❷ **Behaviour:** This means the way you behave – that is what you do when faced with the situation you fear. Especially important is the behaviour of avoiding the situation, either not going into the situation, or getting out of it as quickly as possible.

❸ **Thinking:** This includes your ideas and beliefs, your mental comments to yourself, or your mental pictures about what might happen to you in the situation you fear.

Looking at these parts separately, and learning new skills in each area, is an important part of anxiety management.

■ Anxiety and confidence

Anxiety reduces confidence because it makes it hard to do the things that were once easy. We normally feel confident when we do things well and loose confidence when we fail or avoid situations. It is easy to get into a vicious circle when, because we feel less confidence we avoid a situation, and because we avoid, we feel less confident. Confidence can be regained by learning how to cope better and gradually building up to take on bigger tasks.

 P

Why do anxiety symptoms begin?

There are usually a combination of causes. Two of the important ones are:

❶ **The amount of stress you are under:** You may have a single major problem, or more likely a number of smaller problems which all add up to a large amount of stress. Stress can be measured to some extent by the amount of changes that have taken place in your life recently. Being physically tired, run down and having many changes or traumas makes you more vulnerable to anxiety.

❷ **The kind of person your are:** Some people have a more sensitive emotional nervous system. Their bodies' arousal response might be triggered more quickly and take a longer time to calm down. Some people have learned from their parents in their early experiences how to get anxious and how to worry.

What maintains anxiety?

Why does anxiety stay with you? What keeps it going? Basically, there seem to be two reasons:

❶ Because of the way you behave, especially because you *avoid* the situations you fear.

❷ Because of *beliefs* you have about the situation and its consequences.

Let us look at some examples:

'Lift phobic' people never go in a lift because they may believe it will fall to the bottom of the lift shaft; 'agoraphobics' never go out because they may believe they will collapse and die of a heart attack; some people may avoid meeting others because they believe that in a disagreement, they will lose their temper and hit people; some people obsessively check the locks on the doors and windows over and over before going to bed because they are certain that burglars will break in.

These examples make clear two things:

❶ Thoughts and beliefs can become distorted and exaggerated (and the person may realise that it is just that) about what will happen in the feared situation. Anticipating something bad is going to happen can create a vicious circle of anxiety.

❷ There is often direct avoidance of the feared situation. There may also be a network of 'safety behaviours', such as, always carrying a tranquillizer 'just in case', or always carrying a plastic bag in case of being sick, or always sitting close to the door. All these avoidance behaviours prevent you from truly realising that you can cope with anxiety and that the dangers are not real. Your irrational beliefs continue because they are never proved wrong.

Common myths about anxiety

As anxiety symptoms often occur without any obvious explanation, people often misinterpret them and think there is a more serious problem.

❶ **I'm going crazy:** There is no link between panic anxiety and more serious psychiatric illness.

❷ **I'm going to lose control:** There has never been a recorded case of anybody doing anything 'wild', or 'out of control' or against their wishes.

❸ **I'm having a heart attack:** Although the major symptoms of heart disease include breathlessness and chest pain, the symptoms are generally related to effort and will go away quickly with rest.

❹ **This anxiety will harm me:** Anxiety does not harm you physically, although it is unpleasant and uncomfortable.

❺ **I'm going to faint:** Very unlikely as your heart rate goes up. You only faint if your heart rate and blood pressure drop.

Physical Reaction: The mind becomes focused and preoccupied with the thought 'what is the danger and how can I get to safety'.
Symptom: Panic, preoccupation.

Physical Reaction: The brain sends a biochemical message to the pituitary gland, which releases a hormone which triggers the adrenal gland to release adrenalin.
Symptom: Headaches, dizziness.

Physical Reaction: Pupils dilate.
Symptom: Blurred vision.

Physical Reaction: Mouth becomes dry.
Symptom: Difficulty swallowing.

Physical Reaction: Neck and shoulder muscles tense – large skeletal muscles contract ready for action.
Symptom: Aching neck, backache, headache.

Physical Reaction: Breathing becomes faster and shallower, supplying more oxygen to muscles.
Symptoms: Overbreathing, chest pains, tingling, palpitations, asthma.

Physical Reaction: Heart pumps faster and blood pressure rises.
Symptoms: High blood pressure.

Physical Reaction: Liver releases stored sugar to provide fuel for quick energy.
Symptoms: Excess sugar in blood, indigestion.

Physical Reaction: Adrenalin and noradrenalin are released.

Physical Reaction: Digestion slows down or ceases as blood is diverted away from the stomach.
Symptoms: Nausea, indigestion, ulcers.

Physical Reaction: Muscles at opening of anus and bladder are relaxed.
Symptoms: Frequent urination, diarrhoea.

Physical Reaction: The body cools itself by perspiring: blood vessels and capillaries move close to skin surface.
Symptoms: Excess sweating, blushing.

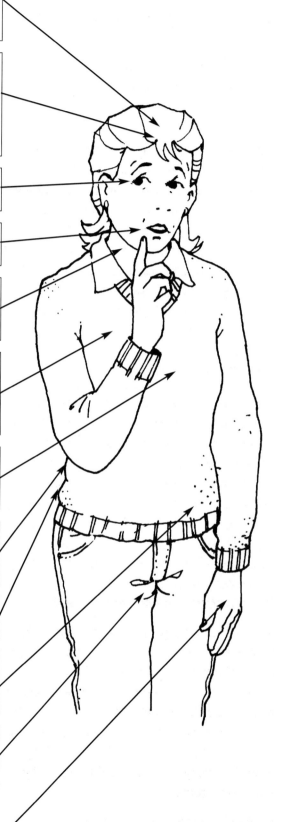

P

'The only thing we have to fear is fear itself'
– Franklin D Roosevelt –

The thoughts we have play a major part in increasing or decreasing our anxiety.

Two examples may make it clearer how thoughts can add to anxiety and lead to it getting out of control.

> Mrs Brown was alarmed to find herself feeling dizzy while waiting at a bus stop. Then she noticed her heart was pounding and her legs felt as if they were giving way. Because the symptoms came out of the blue, she was terrified that she was about to collapse, or even die, and she continued to feel frightened until safely home. After that, just thinking about going out made her feel nervous, and sometimes brought the dizzy feeling back.

> Mr Jones noticed that he felt very tense and irritable when there was a lot of work to be done, and it took him a long time to unwind afterwards. He went to his doctor after starting to get headaches every evening, and although the doctor could not find anything wrong, the patient started to worry that some disease might have been missed. This worry made it even more difficult for him to relax after work.

Although these problems seem quite different, both were caused by a combination of worry and physical tension. Because the feelings did not seem to make any sense, both people started to worry about them, although this only made things worse. They both began to become anxious about being anxious, or to worry more about symptoms than the background stress that originally caused those symptoms.

Research suggests that many people who suffer from anxiety make matters worse for themselves by misinterpreting these physical symptoms. Common misinterpretations include: 'I'm going to have a heart attack', 'I'm going to die', 'I'm going to go completely out of control', 'I'm going to embarrass myself terribly', and 'I am damaging my health'. All these thoughts are very frightening and tend to keep the physical anxiety well stocked up. It must be remembered that these thoughts are also inaccurate distortions of what is actually happening.

The vicious circle of worrying thoughts and physical symptoms is illustrated below:

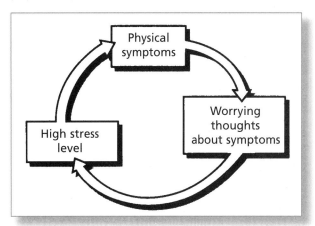

Sometimes we are not fully aware that these frightening thoughts are flashing through our mind. They occur very quickly and often just below the level of consciousness. It is important to try and identify these thoughts and recognise the role they play in creating and maintaining anxiety.

'Present fears are less than horrible imaginings'

– Shakespeare –

Avoidance is an important concept to help us understand why our anxiety is maintained and increases. Take the situation of somebody with agoraphobic tendencies who rushes home after feeling panicky in a supermarket. A number of things happen. First of all their immediate anxiety goes down. Second, the unconscious message stamped in is, 'The only way I can cope with these situations is to avoid them'. Finally, when faced with the same situation – the supermarket – in the future, anxiety will rise quickly and severely.

■ Anxiety curve and avoidance

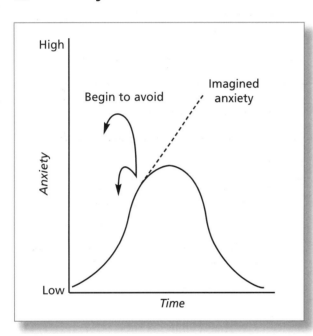

This applies to the agoraphobic with a panic attack, but also applies to the obsessive checker, who avoids anxiety by giving in to the compulsion to check the door locks.

Each time we avoid the situation and our anxiety successfully, we make it more likely that the next time the feared situation crops up, we will avoid it again.

What would happen if you remained in the situation you fear? Would your anxiety increase,

stay the same, or decrease? Most people reply when asked this question 'increase' or 'stay the same'. They generally fear that if their anxiety goes on increasing, something terrible will happen – they will pass out, be sick, collapse, have a heart attack, or go mad. On the graph they imagine the line going up and up and off the page. But this belief is not correct. We know from experience and experiments on anxiety that after a certain time it begins to decrease of its own accord. *If you leave the situation quickly, you will never find this out.*

Avoiding a situation when our anxiety is rising will produce short-term gains – a reduction in anxiety – but long-term pain – our general level of anxiety will increase. Once we start to avoid, the process of 'generalisation' takes place and we begin to avoid more and more situations. It is a slippery slope. The world closes in and we find that our mobility is restricted.

Usually people avoid situations where there is an element of entrapment – or where it is difficult to escape to a place of safety quickly.

Avoidance can often take the subtle form of 'safety behaviours', or habits we get into to make us feel safe. For example, carrying a tranquillizer, 'just in case', carrying a plastic bag, in case we are sick, holding on to something in case we faint, or sitting close to the door. All these behaviours have the effect of depriving us of the knowledge that there is no real danger – we would have coped. For example you might think, 'that was close, if I hadn't had the trolley to hang on to I might have collapsed'. You never learn that you wouldn't collapse if you hang on to the trolley.

The goals of treatment are to equip the anxious person with strategies for controlling anxiety and to encourage them to progressively confront, rather than avoid, situations. In this way you learn, 'I can cope'.

 P

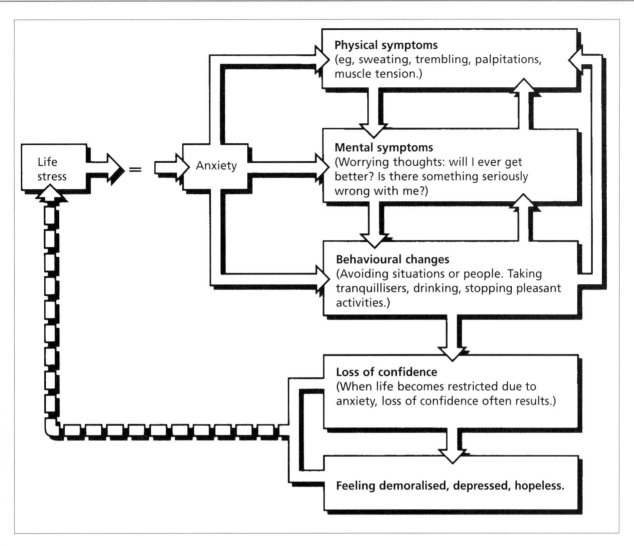

Life stress = Anxiety

Physical symptoms
(eg, sweating, trembling, palpitations, muscle tension.)

Mental symptoms
(Worrying thoughts: will I ever get better? Is there something seriously wrong with me?)

Behavioural changes
(Avoiding situations or people. Taking tranquillisers, drinking, stopping pleasant activities.)

Loss of confidence
(When life becomes restricted due to anxiety, loss of confidence often results.)

Feeling demoralised, depressed, hopeless.

■ What can I do to get better?

❶ Understand the process and how anxiety persists because of a spiralling vicious circle between physical symptoms, worrying thoughts and changes in behaviour.

❷ Break into this vicious circle by learning new skills:

  a *Physical symptoms* can be reduced by learning relaxation or controlled breathing.

  b *Mental symptoms* ie, worry, can be combated by a combination of identifying and challenging worrying thoughts and replacing them with positive ones, and/or distracting yourself.

  c *Behavioural changes* can be altered by deliberately changing your behaviour and going back into difficult situations in a gradual step-by-step fashion.

❸ Make alterations to your lifestyle and so manage successfully the amount of stress you put yourself under. This might involve learning to be more assertive, managing your time better, breaking unhelpful habits or learning other new skills.

'The time to relax is when you don't have any time'

– Sydney Harris –

■ Why is relaxation helpful?

❶ When we are stressed, the muscles in our bodies tense up and this muscular tension causes uncomfortable bodily feelings, such as headache, backache, tight chest and so on.

❷ These aches and pains of tension can cause mental worry, making us even more anxious and tense.

❸ People who are tense often feel tired.

❹ Relaxing slows down the systems in the body that speed up when we get anxious.

❺ If we can learn to turn on the bodily symptoms of relaxation we can turn off the symptoms of tension. They are two sides of the same coin: you can't experience feelings of relaxation and tension at the same time.

■ Relaxation is a skill

The ability to relax is not always something which comes naturally, it is a skill which has to be learnt like playing the piano. The following exercises are designed to help you learn to relax. The Progressive Muscle Relaxation exercise (p11) is quite long and you may obtain a tape of instructions to help you to carry out the routine. When you are able to relax using the first exercise, you can begin to shorten the routine. This should be done gradually until you are able to relax at will, as you need to.

General guidelines

❶ Try to decide in advance when you are going to practice; in this way you can better develop a routine which you can stick to. Make time for yourself.

❷ Make sure that you choose somewhere quiet to exercise, and make sure that no one will disturb you during your practice.

❸ Don't attempt your exercise if you are hungry or have just eaten, or if the room is too hot or too chilly.

❹ Try to adopt a 'passive' attitude, that is, do not worry about your performance or whether you are successfully relaxing. Just 'have a go' and let it happen.

❺ Try to breathe through your nose, using your stomach muscles. Try to breathe slowly and regularly. It is important that you do not take a lot of quick, deep breaths as this can make you feel dizzy or faint and even make your tension worse. When you place your hands on your stomach, you will feel the movement if you are breathing properly. Try this out before you exercise, to make sure that you are used to the feeling.

■ Relaxation in everyday life

❶ Stop rushing around – you achieve more by doing things calmly.

❷ Give yourself short breaks – relax, stretch, go for a walk.

❸ Adopt a relaxed posture. Deliberately relax if you notice yourself tensing up. Drop your shoulders, sit back in your chairs, unclench your fists.

❹ Inject pleasure and treats into your daily routine.

P

This exercise involves tightening and relaxing all the different muscle groups in your body, one at a time. When you tighten a muscle it becomes hard and tightens around the bone, when you relax it loosens, creating a sensation of warm heaviness.

Sit or lie down in a comfortable position. Set aside 15 to 20 minutes with no interruptions or distractions. Relax yourself to the best of your ability. Consider the various muscle groups one at a time, and aim to learn the difference between tight and relaxed muscles. Try constantly to concentrate on the feeling in the muscle as it goes from tight to loose.

Hands and arms
Clench your fists, and tense your arms; feel tightness in your hands and arms, hold for 5 seconds then slowly relax them. Release and relax each muscle group for 10 to 15 seconds. See how far they will go, but do not push. Do not hold on at all; let everything go.

Shoulders
Hunch your shoulders, then gradually let them settle down. Proceed as above.

Forehead
Pull your eyebrows together, then gradually let your forehead smooth out.

Eyes
Screw your eyes up tight, then gradually let them smooth out, leaving your eyes closed, feeling your eyeballs sink, and your eyelids droop. Let them get really heavy.

Jaw
Bite your back teeth together, then gradually ease off, and let your jaw get heavy.

Back of neck
Pull your chin forward on to your chest, feel tightness, then relax.

Front of neck
Pull your chin forward on to your chest, feel tightness, then relax.

Breath
Slow and steady, letting yourself go each time you breathe out.

Tummy
Pull in your tummy tight, then gradually let it go, feeling it relax.

Thighs
Push your heels down hard against the floor, feeling the tightness in your thighs, then gradually let that go.

Calves
Point your toes, then gradually let that tightness go.

Let everything go, further and further, and think about a really relaxing scene, for example, lying in the grass by a river, under a warm sun and a blue sky, or sitting by a fire in a big, comfortable chair. Feel yourself getting heavier and heavier.

Progressive Muscle Relaxation Exercise

Once you can tell the difference between tension and relaxation, you should be able to notice more quickly when your body is getting tense. When this happens, this should be your cue to try any of the following techniques of cued relaxation.

Relax the particular area of your body that feels tense. Tighten the muscles, then relax. Think about that muscle relaxing. Imagine your pulse rate slowing and your whole body slowing down.

Change your posture to a relaxed one when you notice yourself getting tense. Drop your shoulders down in a sideways widening direction.

Repeat a sound or word which you find relaxing, for example, the word 'calm', or say to yourself, 'I am going to relax my body. It is feeling heavier and more relaxed'.

Gaze at a fixed object in the room, such as a picture or ornament which you particularly like.

Think of an image that you find particularly calming and soothing and imagine yourself there, for example, lying on a deserted beach or floating on a feather mattress through the clouds. Imagine the different sights, sounds, smells and sensations. Imagine your body feeling heavier and warmer.

Breathe through your nose and become aware of your breathing. As you breathe out focus on your mental device (from preceding box). Breathe easily, slowly and naturally. Breathe from your stomach, not higher up in your chest.

P

'Life is in the breath'

– Indian Yogi –

Hyperventilation means overbreathing, that is breathing in excess of your body's needs.

Acute hyperventilation is very common during panic attacks. This is understandable because some degree of overbreathing is part of the body's normal response to threat. Recall how when you are suddenly shocked you might gasp. The function of overbreathing is to supply the muscles with more oxygen for 'fight or flight'. It often happens after a combination of strong emotion (fear, excitement, anger etc) and physical exertion, although either can bring it on. If the extra oxygen isn't needed by the muscle, the effect can be dramatic and terrifying and can cause the following symptoms:

◆ rapid breathing, but difficulty in getting breath

◆ tightness in the chest

◆ very rapid heartbeat

◆ sweating

◆ tingling or numbness

◆ feeling of faintness

◆ feeling of unreality

◆ visual problems/blurred vision

◆ rigid muscles, cramps

◆ sudden emotional outbursts, eg, crying

◆ feeling too hot or too cold

When you begin to overbreathe, the balance of gases in the lungs is upset. Breathing in an excess of air too frequently pushes out the carbon dioxide which normally forms a reservoir in the lungs. Because there is too little carbon dioxide in the lungs, the blood becomes more alkaline, which causes the above symptoms. It is important to remember that the symptoms are the effects of too little carbon dioxide.

Two things are necessary: to stop overbreathing, and to get enough carbon dioxide back into the lungs.

A general point to remember is that hyperventilation produces symptoms which are very frightening in themselves. These can cause more overbreathing.

It is very important to break this vicious circle of hyperventilation, leading to frightening secondary symptoms, leading to stress, by learning to control your breathing.

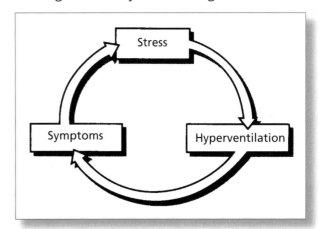

Hyperventilation is not always obvious to the person themself. In many cases hyperventilation can be very subtle, and may be habitual or chronic – going on over a long period of time. This makes the person more vulnerable to panic if placed in a stressful situation which increases the breathing very slightly.

As it is hard work to overbreathe, prolonged periods of hyperventilation will often result in tiredness or exhaustion.

■ Catching it early

If it has happened to you before, you may be able to identify the 'warning signs', for example, a stifling feeling as if the window should be open, tightness in the chest, or noticing your breathing is fast. These should be your cue to:

❶ Stop whatever you are doing and try to find a quiet place to sit down.

❷ Close your eyes and focus on the word 'calm' in your mind.

❸ Try to release some of the tension in the upper body. Sitting in a tense hunched-up position increases the possibility of hyperventilation. Dropping shoulders in a sideways widening direction makes hyperventilation more difficult since the chest and diaphragm muscles are stretched outwards.

❹ Breathe slowly from the stomach, *not* the chest. Breathe in to a count of four slowly and out to a count of four slowly. Or visualise your breathing in as going up one side of a hill, experiencing a plateau at the top, and then breathing out as though coming down the other side. Slow your breathing rate to 10 to 12 breaths per minute.

❺ It may also help to place your hands with your fingertips together on your stomach; make sure that each time you breathe in, your fingertips come apart.

❻ Concentrate on breathing out. Try to breathe through your nose.

■ The re-breathing technique

If your symptoms don't go away after a few minutes it is probable that you haven't caught it quickly enough, and you will need to use the re-breathing technique. This involves breathing in the air you have just breathed out. This air is richer in carbon dioxide and will thus quickly replenish the carbon dioxide you have been exhaling.

◆ Make a mask of your hands and put them over your nose and mouth and keep them there.

◆ Breathe in through your nose (if possible).

◆ Breathe out hard through your mouth.

◆ Breathe your own exhaled air.

◆ This should be done slowly and without holding your breath. Repeat four or five times (no more).

◆ All the time try to stay calm and relaxed.

It is even better to use a paper bag (*not* polythene) over your nose and mouth instead of your hands, if circumstances allow. Adjust your posture so that your elbows are on a level with or above your shoulders. (This makes it difficult to overbreathe.)

■ Recognise hyperventilation

Try to occasionally monitor your breathing rate. Do you breath too deeply or shallowly? Do you sigh and yawn more than others? Triggers for hyperventilation that should be avoided include low blood sugar, tobacco, tea, coffee and other stimulants which accelerate the fight or flight response. Do you breathe in but do not breathe out?

 P

What to do if you are with someone who is hyperventilating

❶ Don't allow yourself to panic. Keep calm, because fear can be infectious.

❷ Familiarise yourself with each of the procedures for controlling hyperventilation. Encourage the person to use the procedures. They may need reminding of what to do, so it may help to talk them through it.

❸ Don't shout or raise your voice. It should be firm but quiet. Speak slowly.

❹ Comfort them physically: a hand gently cupping the back of their neck, or your arm loosely placed around their upper back may be very soothing.

❺ They may become very emotional. Don't get into an argument by disagreeing with what they may be saying. Repeat calming and encouraging statements, such as, 'Just rebreathe your own air . . . you're going to be all right . . . that's it, just drop your shoulders . . . relax'.

❻ Afterwards, treat as if for shock, with rest.

Voluntary hyperventilation

If you find it difficult to believe that the terrifying symptoms experienced during a panic attack can be caused by hyperventilating, try the following experiments.

Exercise 1. Deliberately breathe quickly and deeply through your mouth and nose for 30 seconds and list the symptoms that you experience. It is reassuring to have a paper bag handy for the rebreathing exercise if symptoms are particularly unpleasant. This exercise is useful to show how you can both start and stop, and so control these unpleasant symptoms. This experiment is not dangerous but it is probably more helpful to do it with somebody else.

Exercise 2. Breathe through a straw for one minute. Don't allow any air through your nose; hold your nostrils together.

Rate how unpleasant the sensations are from these exercises and rate how fearful you are. Practice the procedures because the more you consciously provoke the symptoms and then turn them off, the more control you will feel. Try to experience the intensity of the sensation. Fear reduction is accompanied by confronting the things that frighten you.

Thinking about unpleasant symptoms will tend to make them worse. We begin the 'fear of fear' cycle, provoking further symptoms as well as preventing existing ones from disappearing.

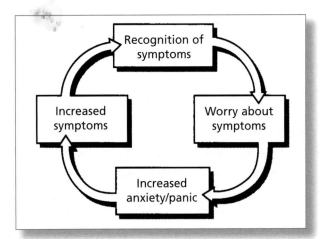

It is difficult simply to turn your attention away from unpleasant feelings. To do so, two things are necessary.

◆ Be determined not to think about or dwell on the symptoms.

◆ Fill your mind with other things; distract yourself.

■ Distraction techniques

❶ **Mental games:** Doing puzzles, crosswords or other word games, reciting a poem, singing a song or counting backwards from one hundred, are all useful distraction exercises. The important thing is that they take your attention away from the panic thoughts.

❷ **Environmental focus:** Concentrating on a specific detail of the world around you, for example, making words out of the number plates of cars or guessing what people do for a living. Focusing on the outside world will prevent you thinking about what is going on inside.

❸ **Using a bridging object:** This might be a photograph or a special brooch or a souvenir from a happy time. Looking at the object generates positive anxiety-reducing thoughts.

❹ **Physical activity:** Giving yourself a task to do takes your mind off worrying thoughts, for example, handing drinks out at a party, changing the music, or washing up after a meal. On a more general level, keeping yourself physically active and mentally distracted from worrying thoughts by pursuing sporting activities is one of the best insulators against stress.

❺ **Meditation:** Techniques derived from eastern mediation systems can also be very useful. Sometimes a *mantra* or a special word can be used. The mediator focuses the mind upon the mantra in an effortless, relaxed way and with practice can block out other thoughts and ideas and achieve a level of relaxation.

❻ **Reading or talking:** Carry a book with you to read or talk to somebody who is with you. Ask somebody to talk to you.

Use distraction to help you get through situations, but try not to allow yourself to fall into the habit of becoming completely dependent on these techniques. After you have successfully coped with the anxiety using these techniques try to gradually do without them.

 P

What is positive self-talk?

Worrying thoughts can make us feel physically anxious (heart racing, muscle tension etc), which then leads to us worrying more. ('Here we go again, I'm going to panic'.) A vicious circle soon gets established, running faster and faster under its own momentum.

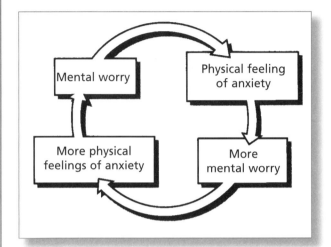

Sometimes we are aware of these thoughts but often we are not. They may take the form of fleeting images or half-formed pictures in our minds. The thoughts tend to flash by automatically and very quickly.

An example may help to make this clearer. Imagine you are running upstairs when you feel a sudden sharp pain in the chest. It gives you a fright, and the thought goes through your head, 'Maybe there's something wrong with my heart'. The thought itself makes you more afraid, your heart beats faster, and the pain seems to take a long time to die away. Later on that day the same thought comes back to you. Once again your heartbeat increases and you feel afraid. The symptoms produced the thought, which made you anxious and added to the symptoms.

Positive self-talk is a copying strategy which involves breaking this vicious circle where negative thoughts lead to increased symptoms. It involves a number of stages.

How to practise positive self-talk

❶ **Find out exactly what you are thinking:** This is not always easy, as thoughts tend to flash through our minds so quickly and automatically that we are not always aware of them. Try writing these thoughts down on a diary sheet. Although it sounds strange, 'think about what you are thinking', or deliberately become 'mindful'.

❷ **Challenge the thoughts for how rational they are:** Research suggests that when people are under stress their thinking can often get distorted. Question your thoughts. Are you exaggerating? Are you thinking in all-or-nothing terms? Are you ignoring the positive?

❸ **Replace negative thoughts with positive ones:** After you have challenged your existing thoughts, rewrite them in a more positive realistic language. Straighten out those distorted thoughts. It is sometimes useful to carry these positive challenges around with you on an index card.

■ Preparation

It's not going to be as bad as I think.

It won't last long and I can cope with it.

I am getting better and need to go to rebuild my confidence.

If I do get bad feelings, I know they won't last long and I can cope with them.

It's better to go than not to go. Worry doesn't help.

I might enjoy it if I go.

■ Coping

Concentrate on what is going on.

I can tolerate anxiety; I've managed it many times before.

Remember to relax and think positive.

This is just anxiety; it is an unpleasant feeling but I've never been ill.

Concentrate on what I have to do.

I know I am going to be OK.

The feelings are unpleasant but not harmful or dangerous.

One step at a time.

The feelings *always* pass away.

■ Praise/Review

I can be pleased with the progress I'm making.

I achieved that; I'm getting better.

I coped with that.

I did that well.

If I keep this up I'm going to get really good at this.

I handled that; it should be easier next time.

P

What is the evidence?
What evidence do I have to support my thoughts?
What evidence do I have against them?

What alternative views are there?
How would someone else view this situation?
How would I have viewed this situation in the past?

What is the effect of thinking the way I do?
Does it help me, or hinder me from getting what I want? How?

What thinking error am I making?

a   Am I thinking in all-or-nothing terms
    ignoring the middle ground?

b   Am I awfulising or catastrophising
    overestimating the chances of disaster?

c   Am I personalising
    blaming myself for something which is not my fault?

d   Am I focusing on the negative
    looking on the dark side; ignoring my strengths?

e   Am I jumping to conclusions
    predicting the future and mind-reading?

f   Am I living by fixed rules
    fretting about how things ought to be; overusing the words should, must and can't?

What action can I take?
What can I do to change my situation? Am I overlooking solutions to problems on the assumption they won't work?

What is the worst possible outcome?
What is the worst thing that can happen and how bad would that really be?

This technique is useful for unearthing and exploring hidden assumptions behind your thoughts. Start with a thought and try and follow it back into your psyche finding what is behind each thought. Pose some of the following questions. What would be so bad about that? What might happen? What would that mean? Why?

The example below is a true example of a woman who had a lift phobia for 20 years but had never unravelled her thoughts to find what she was really scared of. She was actually quite surprised at what she found, and recognised that her fantasy at the end of her chain of thoughts was completely irrational.

Thought	Rational challenge
Going into a lift would be absolutely awful.	It would make me really anxious.
Why would it be upsetting? I don't know. I can't bear even to think about it.	Close your eyes. Think what might happen – these are only my thoughts.
What might happen? I'd press the wrong button and the lift would jam between floors.	It's possible but I'd estimate chances of that happening as one in five thousand.
What would be so bad about that? Well that would be the end – I'd go crazy.	It wouldn't be the end. I'd get panicky but people can't go mad from being frightened.
Why? Because I'd be stuck in the lift, unable to get out.	It's a glass-fronted lift in a busy store; they'd notice me and get me out.
How long might you be stuck? Well, maybe a couple of days.	That's an over-estimation – maybe 30 minutes at most.
What would be so bad about that? I wouldn't have any food or water.	They would have got me out. If not, I wouldn't want food, or they would pass it to me.
What would that mean? I'd starve – by the time they found me I'd be a withered skeleton, huddled in the corner.	Nobody starves in two days – I would not be a skeleton.

 P

Please make an entry whenever you notice a definite increase in anxiety.

Diary Sheet

DATE/ TIME	DESCRIPTION OF SITUATION	ANXIETY LEVEL: 0–10	DESCRIPTION OF A PHYSICAL FEELINGS B THOUGHTS	COPING METHOD	ANXIETY LEVEL AFTER: 0–10

'My life has been full of terrible misfortunes, most of which never happened'
– Montaigne –

❶ Pinpoint the worrying thought: Worrying thoughts are often the result of half-formed ideas chasing each other around in your mind. This vicious circle can be broken by identifying and airing the worrying thought. Write down your top five worrying thoughts. Bringing them out into the open relieves the pressure.

❷ Look at the evidence: What is the evidence? Instead of assuming that your thought is true, examine the actual evidence. Write down on a sheet of paper the evidence for both sides of the argument. What is the probability that your thought is correct? Rate the thought on a percentage scale (0%–100%) in terms of how much you actually now believe it. For example, 'I am useless at this job' . . . Believability = 30%.

❸ Explore the worst possible outcome: What is the worst thing that can happen? Fantasy is usually worse than reality. Imagine walking into a dark deep cave. You might feel frightened because you would not be able to see what is stretching ahead of you. Then imagine turning on a powerful torch which shines on the walls, showing the limits of the cave. More often than not our fantasies are much worse than a clearly identified worst option. Once we have placed limits on our worries, by identifying the worst possible outcome, they are easier to deal with.

❹ Put yourself in somebody else's shoes: What alternative views are there? How would someone else view this situation? Think of two or three significant people in your life and imagine how they would view this situation? Talk to yourself out loud. What advice would they give?

❺ Cost-benefit analysis: What is the effect of thinking the way I do? Ask yourself. How will holding this thought help me and how will it hurt me? List the advantages and disadvantages of holding a particular negative thought.

❻ Think in shades of grey: Am I thinking in all or nothing terms, or seeing things in a black or white fashion? Are you thinking of yourself as either 'a total success', or 'a total failure'. This common style of distorted thinking misses out on the middle ground, the grey area between the black and white. Remind yourself that things are usually somewhere between 0% and 100%, and rate where your negative thought is on that scale.

❼ Box your worries in: If you are constantly plagued by worrying, set aside a specific time of twenty minutes as 'dedicated worry time'. Tackle each worry as a problem to think hard about and solve. If you find yourself worrying at other times during the day, postpone that worry until the allotted time.

❽ Keep perspective: Compare the present problem with other really important issues in your life. For example, say that you are worrying because you are stuck in a traffic jam and are going to be late for a meeting. How does this compare with the worst upsetting time in your life, for example, when your mother was critically ill.

❾ Visualise yourself ten years after: Will this worry matter in ten years time? Imagine that you are ten years older and are looking back to this time in your life. How important will this concern be in the long term? Looked at from a distance mountains can appear as molehills.

❿ Turn worry into action: Ask yourself: Is there anything that I can do about this? Is there anything I can do to change the situation? Make a list of the things you could do. Worry is only useful when it spurs you on to solve problems.

⓫ Distract yourself: If you have reached the conclusion that there is nothing that you can do, then distract yourself with some absorbing activity. Our minds only have a limited capacity so if you start thinking about something else you can crowd out those worrying thoughts. Distraction can work on a macro level, where you might alter your lifestyle or take up a hobby. Distraction can also work on a micro level where you can take your mind off worrying thoughts by playing mental games, or focusing on a specific detail of your environment.

P

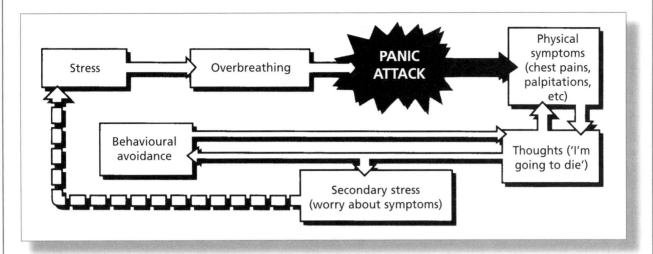

■ What is a panic attack?

Panic attacks are common, occurring in up to five per cent of the general population. They are defined by a sudden onset of intense apprehension, fear or terror accompanied by physical symptoms such as;

- ◆ difficulty in breathing
- ◆ dizziness
- ◆ palpitations
- ◆ chest pains
- ◆ tingling sensations
- ◆ shaking
- ◆ sweating
- ◆ visual difficulty
- ◆ feelings of unreality
- ◆ jelly legs

The thoughts that accompany these symptoms often include; 'I'm going to lose control', 'I'm going mad', 'I'm going to die', 'I'm going to have a heart attack' or 'I'm going to embarrass myself'. Although it is perhaps understandable to experience these thoughts, they are largely mistaken and are misinterpretations of what is actually going on. Unfortunately, once you start thinking these thoughts, you become more anxious, keeping the bodily symptoms going. An upwardly spiralling vicious circle of thoughts and physical symptoms is created.

The situation is further complicated by the fact that when most people have a panic attack,

their natural reaction is to try and leave the situation they are in as quickly as possible. This avoidance brings temporary relief, but increases the likelihood of further apprehension, negative thoughts, bodily symptoms and the development of a phobic reaction.

■ A symptom of stress

Panic attacks are one of the symptoms of a build-up of stress. This symptom is perhaps more frightening than nausea, headaches or diarrhoea but in some ways it is a similar reaction. People who experience panic attacks seem to be those who experience stress in their respiratory and cardiovascular system rather than in their muscular or gastrointestinal systems.

Very often the symptom of panic produces such worry and stress that these symptoms become more of a problem than the original stresses that caused them.

The body's fear reaction and how it becomes oversensitive

The symptoms are in fact an exaggeration of the normal bodily reaction to a fearful situation. Imagine what would happen if you were up a ladder and felt it slip from under you. Your heart would pound, your breathing would alter, you might turn very pale or break out in a sweat. However, as soon as you climbed down the ladder and recognised that you were safe, but had nearly had a nasty accident, your anxiety would die down. You would understand the symptoms as being quite natural, and you would not worry about those symptoms. But what if you experienced exactly those same symptoms pushing a trolley around a supermarket or sitting at your desk at work? Your mind would immediately try to make sense of the situation and would come up with a number of very frightening thoughts.

The problem with panic attacks is that your fear reaction has become oversensitive and is being triggered in a variety of apparently normal situations. This oversensitivity of the fear reaction is more likely if you are tired or under a lot of stress. Sometimes this stress can be caused by worrying about having another panic attack. If you have had one bad attack you can become over-vigilant, an expert at detecting the normal changes in your body which you would usually ignore. You are constantly on the look-out for slight changes that may indicate that something is amiss. Once you begin to imagine something is wrong, you become slightly frightened, triggering the body's reaction and the vicious circle of panic takes off. Other factors which can trigger panics include physical exertion, hunger, hormonal changes, caffeine and alcohol.

Can panic feelings harm me?

No. No one can die of fright. Though panic feelings are unpleasant they cannot in any way harm you. The feelings themselves are quite normal. It is just that they are happening in an ordinary situation, rather than in an obviously dangerous or frightening one. You are not going mad or having a heart attack, although these are common fears. It is almost impossible to faint while you are having a panic attack, because your blood pressure is higher and not lower than normal as your heart is racing. People usually only faint when their blood pressure drops. The one exception to this is a blood or injury phobia.

Summary of main points about panic attacks

❶ A panic attack is the same as the body's normal fear reaction, but it is happening in an ordinary situation.

❷ Your body's normal fear reaction has become oversensitive and has become easily triggered. This happens particularly if you are tired or under stress, but this reaction can be triggered by exertion, hormonal changes, hunger, caffeine or alcohol.

❸ The feelings themselves are not harmful and do not indicate that there is anything seriously wrong with you.

❹ The feelings can be caused and maintained by a combination of worrying thoughts, hyperventilation or overbreathing, and avoidance of situations that create anxiety.

❺ Once you understand what is going on, half the battle is won.

 P

1 *Remember panic feelings are only normal reactions that are exaggerated – they are not dangerous.*

2 *They are not harmful and nothing worse will happen. The feelings will soon pass.*

3 *Notice what is happening in your body now. Stay with the present. Slow down, relax, but keep going.*

4 *Thinking about what might happen is unhelpful. Only now matters.*

5 *Accept the feelings. Let them run through you and they will disappear more quickly. Try not to fight the panic. Float over it.*

6 *Monitor your level of anxiety: 10 (worst) to 0 (least). Watch the level go down.*

7 *Stay in the situation. If you run away, avoid or escape, it will be more difficult in the future.*

8 *Take a few slow, deep breaths. Breath from your stomach – say the word 'calm' as you breath out.*

9 *Consciously relax your tense muscles. Feel yourself relaxing. Drop your shoulders.*

10 *Now begin to concentrate again on what you were doing before. Slowly move on when ready.*

Ten Rules for Coping with Panic

'Feel the fear and do it anyway'

– Susan Jefferies –

Avoiding anything that makes us anxious is in some ways a natural reaction. However, avoiding some situations that create anxiety can lead to the development of phobias and loss of confidence. Once we begin to avoid things, we may find our mobility becomes increasingly restricted.

When you either stay in the situation you fear, or deliberately put yourself in that position, your anxiety will go up, reach a plateau and then go down again. The first time you do this the anxiety will take time to subside. The second time you face the situation you fear, your anxiety will be less severe and fall in a shorter time. Each time you put yourself into that situation your anxiety will progressively be less severe and die away more quickly. The diagram below shows how this anxiety hill gets smaller and smaller.

The best way of overcoming avoidance and loss of confidence is by tackling your fears one step at a time in easy stages. This technique is called graded practice or systematic desentisation. By identifying situations which you avoid, and gradually confronting them time and again, you can reduce the anxiety associated with those situations. It is important to practice easier tasks first, so as to build up your confidence before tackling more difficult situations.

When you confront the anxiety-provoking situation be prepared. Be armed with a relaxation technique, understand about breathing control, and have a number of positive self statements you can repeat to yourself. Expect some anxiety – do not expect to feel no anxiety; but you can be sure that if you carry on confronting your anxiety it *will* go down.

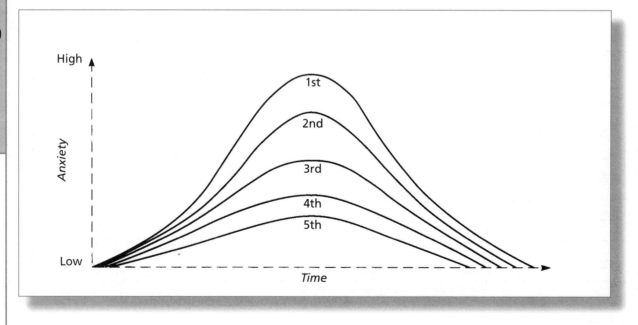

P

❶ List a number of situations which you avoid because of your anxiety.

❷ Describes the situations in as much detail as possible. Be specific. Rather than saying, 'Going on a bus', say, 'Travelling, alone on the number 29 bus, into town, on a weekday afternoon'.

❸ Rate how much anxiety you anticipate each situation will create on a scale of 0–10 where 0 = low anxiety, 5 = moderate anxiety and 10 = extreme anxiety.

❹ Rearrange the situations in ranked order with the most difficult at the top.

❺ Start with the easiest situation and practice it. If practice is to be helpful it must be **a** regular, **b** frequent, **c** prolonged – you must go on practising until the anxiety has died down. Practice each situation 3–4 times.

❻ If something is too hard, look at ways of breaking it down into intermediate stages.

❼ Do not be put off by feeling anxious. Remember you are learning to master anxiety rather than avoid it.

❽ Reward yourself for your successes.

❾ Keep a record of how you have coped.

Example
Going into a lift in a department store, on my own, on a weekday afternoon.

$\boxed{6}$

Catching the number 29 bus to the station, on my own, on Saturday morning.

$\boxed{5}$

YOUR TARGETS	ANXIETY RATING 0 TO 10
1 (Most difficult)	
2	
3	
4	
5	
6	
7	
8	
9	
10	

■ Why do I feel good one day and bad the next?

Everybody's moods go up and down. Sometimes we have a good day, sometimes we have a bad day. Very often these changes in mood are so small we don't notice them. When you have been feeling anxious or depressed you are sensitised to your own reactions. You are on the look-out for any minor changes that might occur. When normal fluctuations occur, which you may have paid little attention to previously, you notice them. This attention with its associated worrying thoughts means that those minor changes become exaggerated and magnified. Your mood tends to go up and down like a roller coaster with high peaks and low troughs.

To counteract this tendency, first you have to recognise that it is happening. Then watch out for your thoughts. Are you allowing 'all-or-nothing thinking' or 'catastrophising' to take place? Do you think when the day starts badly, 'Oh no, today's going to be terrible, I might as well not bother. I'm not getting any better'? Challenge that thought and change it to, 'It's just a bad day, no more, or less. Everybody has them.'

■ How long do I need to keep practice going?

Sometimes when people confront a fear or phobia they expose themselves to the anxiety-provoking situation once or twice and say 'I'm cured, I've cracked it', and then stop putting themselves back into that situation. Research suggests that for a fear to be truly banished, you have to return regularly to the avoided situation, otherwise there is a tendency for the fear to return. So, keep practice going. Watch out for subtle avoidance when you say to yourself, 'I've done it once, I'm OK now, I don't need to do it again.'

■ Dealing with setbacks

Expect setbacks and you won't be disappointed. Most people will have setbacks; the important thing is not to be demoralised. Be aware of saying to yourself: 'I'm fine now, everything is OK'. Even when you are doing well expect a setback – plan for it. When it occurs don't be demoralised; it is likely to be one step back but three steps forward. Setbacks come to instruct.

■ Are you looking after yourself?

Are you getting enough fun out of life? When we are under stress the pleasurable activities get squeezed out by everyday life. Hobbies get dropped, we see friends less often. It is important to reverse this process and restart the things that you used to enjoy. Make a list of all the things you used to enjoy in the past and push yourself into restarting some of these activities. Treat yourself occasionally.

 P

Stress is the result of an imbalance between the demands made on us and our personal resources to deal with these demands.

The balance between a person's resources and the demands being made on them can be compared with a bank account. If too many demands are made on the account we go into the 'red' and become overdrawn, which is comparable to being under stress. In normal circumstances we can cope with the everyday demands of life such as maintenance of job and relationships, which is comparable with the way routine standing orders regularly diminish our financial account. It is only when extra stresses or demands come along that we can tip over 'into the red'. Sometimes a crisis may be the result of a 'last straw' which just tips the balance and we fall 'into the red' or stress.

■ Recommendations

❶ Some stress is good for you. Identify your own resources and situations which you find stressful. Learn to identify your own optimal level of stress and do not be pressurised beyond it.

❷ Anticipate stress by balancing your demands and resources in advance. Decide what is important – have priorities.

❸ When experiencing stress make sure that you:

◆ Do not withdraw from social support;

◆ Keep communicating – ventilate your feelings;

◆ Keep areas and times for relaxation.

❹ Reduce demands:

◆ Do not expect too much of yourself;

◆ Do not feel that you have to live up to others' expectations of you;

◆ Think twice about how important tasks are. Try saying 'No';

◆ Break your goals into manageable proportions;

◆ Think positively about your abilities.

Stress Control

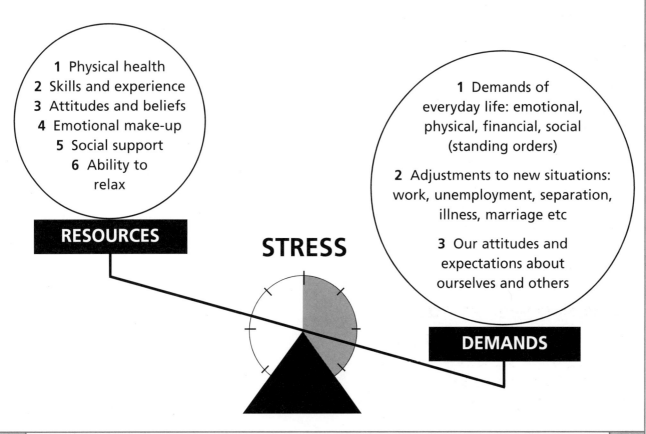

1 Physical health
2 Skills and experience
3 Attitudes and beliefs
4 Emotional make-up
5 Social support
6 Ability to relax

RESOURCES

STRESS

1 Demands of everyday life: emotional, physical, financial, social (standing orders)

2 Adjustments to new situations: work, unemployment, separation, illness, marriage etc

3 Our attitudes and expectations about ourselves and others

DEMANDS

'Sleep . . . balm of hurt minds . . . chief nourisher in life's feast'

– Macbeth –

■ Useful information about sleeping

❶ There is no such thing as an ideal length of sleep. Some people need 10 hours, others need three. Napoleon, Churchill and Margaret Thatcher are all reported as only needing between three and four hours a night.

❷ As you grow older you require less sleep. A person who had 10 hours at 20 years old may require five or less at 60.

❸ There is no danger in losing a few nights sleep. People often assume they will become ill, or their performance will be impaired. Both fears are usually groundless.

❹ Your body will take all the sleep it needs unless forcibly prevented.

❺ Research into insomnia finds that people with sleeping difficulties consistently over-estimate how long it takes them to get to sleep and how much sleep they have had. The next day they are usually oversensitised to bodily symptoms, interpreting them as signs of tiredness.

■ Hints for getting to sleep

❶ Prepare yourself before going to bed:

◆ Take exercise early in the day;

◆ Avoid spicy or heavy food and caffeine in the few hours before you retire;

◆ Have a milky drink before bed;

◆ Take time to relax by having a warm bath or listening to restful music, or complete a relaxation exercise;

◆ Make sure your bedroom is quiet and your bed is comfortable.

❷ Go to bed only when you are sleepy; do not try to get more sleep by going to bed early.

❸ Use your bed only for sleeping. Do not read, watch television or eat in bed unless you are sure by your past experience that these activities help you to sleep.

❹ When you are in bed, relax and do not think about worrying issues. If there is a problem, identify all your worrying thoughts by writing them down on a piece of paper earlier in the evening, and leave that piece of paper downstairs. If you are still worrying write down your worries. Then try to think about pleasant things.

❺ Distract yourself by playing mental games, such as remembering the names of your classmates at school, counting football teams in the league, or counting prime numbers.

❻ Carry out a muscle relaxation exercise. As you lie in bed tighten up and relax muscle groups in your body.

❼ If you have not fallen asleep in about 15 to 20 minutes, or if you wake up and cannot get back to sleep, then get out of bed and do something else until you feel sleepy. Don't lie there tossing and turning. Go to a different room and do something which is different and unstimulating like reading, or ironing. Return to bed after a break when you feel sleepy.

❽ Set your alarm and get up at the same time each morning regardless of how much sleep you received during the night.

❾ Turn the clock face away so you cannot see what time it is.

❿ Do not catnap during the day. Try to establish a regular routine for going to bed and getting up.

 P

■ Advantages and disadvantages of using tranquillisers

Advantages

❶ Tranquillisers make you less anxious in the short term.

❷ They can help you to tackle difficult situations which otherwise you might avoid.

❸ They work quite quickly, having an effect on the nervous system in about 10 to 15 minutes.

Disadvantages

❶ Tranquillisers do not cure the problems of anxiety. They only mask the symptoms, and do not deal with the original causes.

❷ By the very act of taking a tranquilliser you are avoiding coping on your own. This erodes your self-confidence.

❸ There is a strong possibility that long-term use of tranquillisers will create dependency and addiction.

❹ Tranquillisers have physical side-effects: drowsiness, appetite changes, dry mouth, dizziness, poor coordination.

■ Advice for coming off tranquillisers

❶ Work out a programme of gradual reduction with your family doctor, lasting for a couple of months or even longer.

❷ Sometimes there are side-effects of withdrawal which are very similar to anxiety symptoms. It is important to remember that they are *not* the original anxiety symptoms returning, although the symptoms seem similar.

❸ Take one day at a time. Tell yourself you are coping with just the next day, or even just the next hour. Talk to yourself positively. Remind yourself that the symptoms will not last for ever, and that they are not harmful.

❹ Keeping active and occupied will take your mind off the stress of withdrawal. Plan pleasant distracting activities.

❺ Use your anxiety management skills and become more confident in controlling your anxiety.

❻ Identify the time of day and week when it would be easier to miss out on a tablet or a portion of a tablet; this is the best place to start.

❼ Don't try to come off everything all at once. Plan a gradual and even reduction.

'To a man who is afraid everything rustles'

– Sophocles –

■ What is agoraphobia?

Agoraphobia is a condition characterised by a complex mixture of fears, anxieties and avoidances. The syndrome has occurred throughout history; the word *agoraphobia* comes from the Greek and literally means 'fear of the marketplace'. More recent research indicates that people with agoraphobia have a fear of panic or anxiety, regardless of where they occur. The secondary fear is the fear of situations, such as a crowded place, or a situation of entrapment.

The agoraphobic person usually experiences unpleasant physical symptoms of anxiety, mainly panic attacks. Some people have nervous systems which are more prone to having panic attacks. The person is inclined to worry about these attacks and to misinterpret their significance. Common thoughts are: 'I'm going to die', or 'I'm going to have a heart attack', 'I'm going to faint', 'I'm going to lose control of my bowels or bladder', 'I'm going mad'. Following this experience, the person starts to avoid situations associated with these attacks. Situations which tend to be avoided are those that have an element of 'entrapment', and those that are a long way from a place of safety.

■ A vicious circle

The initial panic attack or experience of anxiety usually comes out of the blue, but behind it there are often a number of underlying stresses. The person may be tired, or run down, or may just 'have a lot on their plate'.

After the first panic attack, a familiar vicious circle is likely to occur. The individual worries about having another attack, and is naturally inclined to avoid certain situations. This worry and avoidance makes future attacks more likely. The result is a loss of confidence and a feeling of insecurity. The more insecure the individual feels the more he or she is likely to avoid situations; thus, the vicious circle gets established. Often the person can feel trapped within a 'spiders's web' of avoidance.

Very often the person with agoraphobia is in an environment where people allow them to avoid. These significant people may think that they are being kind but they are not. Sometimes the partner or relative may be getting something positive from the situation. They might feel stronger and more needed as the agoraphobic feels weaker and more dependent.

The key features in reversing this vicious downward spiral are:

❶ Understanding what is really going on.

❷ Learning to gain some control over anxiety symptoms by acquiring new skills, such as relaxation, breathing exercises, distraction, and positive self-talk.

❸ Progressively confronting the situations previously avoided, in a graded manner.

❹ Notice your confidence growing as you successfully manage more difficult situations. Build on this confidence – change your lifestyle.

P

Social phobia is a fear of being scrutinised, evaluated or the centre of attention. Underlying this fear is the idea that the person will be evaluated negatively – people will think that they are strange or incompetent. It may be that the person with the social phobia believes that people will see that they are anxious, or that they will say something embarrassing, or make a mistake or that some aspect of their appearance will attract criticism. They often fear situations including public speaking, writing in public, eating or drinking in public or even using public toilets. Social situations are endured rather than enjoyed. The person may be prone to panic attacks and avoidance behaviour. It is estimated that about 5 per cent of the population have some element of social phobia.

The cause of social phobia is largely the same as any other phobia. Some people may have a more reactive nervous system, coupled with experiences in childhood where social situations were anxiety provoking and often avoided. People who are sensitive to criticism or overly concerned with 'creating a good impression' may be more susceptible to social phobia.

■ Treatment of social phobia

There are five elements to the treatment of social phobia.

❶ Learning to control anxiety and panic through relaxation exercises, hyperventilatory control, distraction, and positive self-talk.

❷ Correcting faulty and distorted thinking patterns and beliefs.

❸ Gradually increasing involvement in social situations through a programme of graded exposure. Confront situations, drop safety behaviours.

❹ Being more assertive. 'This is me – this is what I think – this is how I feel. I'm OK.' – build confidence.

❺ Reduce self-consciousness – focus on others rather than yourself.

■ Distorted thinking patterns

The person with the social phobia often worries about situations, focuses inwards, starts to avoid, loses confidence and then worries and avoids more.

A classic vicious circle of worry, anxiety and avoidance.

❶ The person with social phobia usually over-estimates the extent that other people will notice their anxiety. Most people do not pay a great deal of attention to other people that they don't know. If the social phobic blushes in front of ten people, they will assume most of the people noticed, whereas in reality maybe one or two might have.

❷ They will then over-estimate the negative evaluation that other people will make. If someone did notice somebody else blushing the chances are that they would not make a negative evaluation at all. Most people that you know have already made their minds up about your character and are not going to have an extreme shift in opinion on the basis of one event.

❸ Social phobics often have one set of rules for themselves and one for other people. If asked whether they would evaluate somebody negatively whom they saw being anxious or blushing or shaking they would usually say no! However, they assume that other people will evaluate them negatively. The person with social phobia needs to recognise these distorted thinking patterns.

'They will see that I am anxious'

'If they see I am anxious they will wonder why'

'They might think I am odd and peculiar'

'They might mention it to others'

'They probably dislike me because of my anxiety'

'They may wonder why I'm so anxious and even think I'm weak or inept.'

A simple phobia refers to an isolated experience of anxiety attached to a particular object or situation. It is different from a complex phobia where there are multiple fears and anxieties. Simple phobias are often of animals, such as spiders, snakes, cats and dogs; or illness and blood; or natural phenomena such as thunderstorms, lightning, wind, or heights; more unusually they can be of situations such as eating or even going to the toilet in a public place.

The characteristics of a simple phobia are:

❶ An intense fear of an object or situation, which is out of all proportion to the situation which evokes it.

❷ The person recognises that it is unreasonable and irrational but cannot do anything about it.

❸ Sufferers avoid the feared situation as much as possible and this process of avoidance interferes with the smooth running of their everyday life.

It is estimated that the incidence of phobia in the general population is between 2–3 per cent. The specific phobias often have their origins in childhood fears which have failed to diminish with time. When looking at the development and maintenance of phobias, a number of factors appear relevant. There is often a family history of fear, phobia and avoidance; parents can often act as models for their children. If they are not acting as direct models, it is possible that they are subtly supporting the child's avoidance behaviour. Often there is a traumatic experience which acts as the nucleus for the subsequent phobia. But the main factor which keeps phobia going is a marked pattern of avoidance behaviour. Avoidance reduces the immediate feeling of anxiety, which strengthens the likelihood of avoidance in future.

The treatment of choice for a simple phobia has a number of components:

❶ Understanding the process, development and maintenance of the phobia.

❷ Gaining some control over physical reactions of fear and anxiety, through relaxation training, breathing exercises, distraction and positive self-talk.

❸ Constructing a desensitisation hierarchy of situations which the person is afraid of. This is done by rating specific situations on a scale of 0–10, where 0 = no anxiety and 10 is equal to the worst possible anxiety. Be as specific and concrete as possible in describing situations.

❹ Once a hierarchy is established, start at the bottom and work up by exposing yourself to the situation. This gradual exposure can sometimes be done in imagination and paired with a state of relaxation. The golden rule is that ultimately the only way to overcome a phobia is to face it directly. Stay in the situation of fear until you notice your anxiety going down. Once you feel comfortable with one situation move on to the next most difficult one.

◼ Example of desensitisation hierarchy

❶ Look at picture of spider.

❷ Watch video of spider.

❸ Stay in same room as spider in a jar.

❹ Pick up jar with spider in it.

❺ Open lid of jar and look at spider.

❻ Put spider in bucket – look at it.

❼ Touch spider in bucket.

❽ Put spider on desk.

❾ Touch spider on desk.

❿ Let spider walk on hand.

P

Obsessive compulsive disorders (OCD) usually have two aspects. First, obsessive thoughts which intrude repeatedly into the mind against the will, despite all attempts to banish them. These thoughts may concern contaminating oneself or others, harming others, going against a social taboo, or some other harm occurring. Secondly, these thoughts are often accompanied by 'compulsions' or 'rituals' which are acts that are carried out time and again, to reduce anxiety, although the person may know that they are silly and try to resist them. These acts may include frequent hand washing, checking, hoarding or carrying out special rituals.

These types of difficulty tend to occur in people who have always had meticulous and perfectionist personalities, although they can occur in anybody. Such tendencies can get worse or flare up during times of personal stress or change.

The symptoms are extremely distressing and can end up dominating a person's life. Avoidance of certain situations or objects that trigger anxiety is common. While this seems a reasonable short-term strategy it actually adds to the long-term problem. Anxiety about the symptoms is likely to make the symptoms worse. Intrusive thoughts about harming others can at times be bizarre and frightening but the risk of translating the thoughts into action is in fact almost nonexistent.

■ Treatment of OCD

❶ Identify and talk about all of your symptoms no matter how embarrassing they are.

❷ It is helpful to carefully monitor and identify when and how often these thoughts and behaviours occur. Keep a diary sheet.

❸ Learn new techniques for controlling anxiety symptoms such as relaxation, distraction and positive self-talk.

❹ As with any phobia, you will need to expose yourself gradually to the situation that you fear. For example, if you have a fear of contamination, touch dirty objects.

❺ Once you have deliberately made yourself anxious by confronting the fear, you need to manage your anxiety and resist the compulsive behaviour. This third phase is called 'response prevention' and may mean resisting handwashing or checking activities.

❻ Most OCD suffers try to avoid thinking about their intrusive thoughts. Often the more you try to push these thoughts out the more they bounce back into consciousness. Try deliberately thinking about the thought for 10 minutes a day.

❼ Do not confuse a thought with an action. 'A thoughtie is not a naughty'.

❽ Set limits on your rituals and compulsions. Cut down the frequency.

❾ Put a rubber band around your wrist and every time you think of the unwanted thought tweak yourself.

❿ Identify the stresses in your life that are presently exacerbating your symptoms. Change your lifestyle.

⓫ Very often the whole family may be involved in the maintenance of these rituals and may be asked to give reassurance, which temporarily dampens down your anxiety. They have to learn not to give this reassurance and say something neutral: 'You know they said at the hospital that I was not to answer those questions'.

⓬ Explore the significance of the concept of responsibility in your life and how it fits in with your symptoms. Do you feel overly responsible?

⓭ If symptoms are severe, medication that has a specific effect on the serotonin levels in your brain can be helpful.

Three Rules to Remember

Repeat your fears until bored to tears.
When fears are faced they get erased.
I must refrain to untrain my brain.

■ **Rate the following statements reflecting your experiences over the last two weeks**

0	1	2	3	4	5
Not Troublesome		Moderately Troublesome		Very Troublesome	

THOUGHTS   **RATING**

1	I fear that I may harm others.	
2	I fear that I may harm myself.	
3	I have very violent or horrific images.	
4	I fear blurting out obscenities or insults.	
5	I fear that I will be responsible for something terrible happening.	
6	I am concerned with contamination by dirt or gems.	
7	I am concerned with environmental contamination (eg, radiation).	
8	I am concerned with bodily waste and secretion.	
9	I have forbidden all perverse sexual thoughts, images and impulses.	
10	I worry about my sexual behaviour towards others.	
11	I am very concerned about saving and hoarding certain things.	
12	I am very concerned with religious matters.	
13	I am very concerned with sacrilege and blasphemy.	
14	I am very concerned with the need for exactness and symmetry.	
15	I often have 'magical' or unseen thoughts about things happening.	
16	I am very concerned with illness and disease.	
17	I am very concerned with parts of my body and aspects of my appearance.	
18	I am very bothered by certain sounds and noise.	
Any other obsessional thoughts:		
19		
20		

BEHAVIOUR   **RATING**

1	I carry out excessive, ritualised handwashing/bathing/grooming.	
2	I carry out excessive cleaning of household items.	
3	I compulsively check locks and appliances.	
4	I repeatedly check that I have not made a mistake.	
5	I frequently need to repeat routine activities (eg, in/out/up/down from chair).	
6	I frequently find myself counting, ordering or arranging things excessively.	
7	I am prone to hoard or collect certain items.	
8	I have certain mental rituals I carry out.	
Any other compulsive behaviour or things you avoid:		
9		
10		

 P

Name _____ **Date** _____

OBSESSIONAL THOUGHTS

Identify the three most troublesome, intrusive thoughts that you would like
to work on:

1

2

3

COMPULSIONS/RITUALS

Identify the three most noticeable compulsions or rituals that you would like to alter or
resist:

1

2

3

AVOIDANCE

Identify three situations that you deliberately avoid so as to reduce your
anxiety:

1

2

3

What is health anxiety?

People with health anxiety, or hypochondriasis, tend to experience excessive psychological reactions to perceived physical symptoms or bodily functions. For example, the individual may notice a small pain or a mole and they will think that all is not well with their bodies. They will experience the symptom as evidence of some serious illness, such as cancer, a brain tumour, or impending heart failure. Most people would simply ignore these symptoms and they would go away. The person with health anxiety will focus on the symptom, become physically anxious, and usually will seek reassurance often from medical services. A vicious circle of worry occurs and the more they worry, the more they notice physical symptoms of anxiety which are misinterpreted as indicators of a serious illness (see diagram).

This type of worry tends to occur as frequently in males as females and usually begins in their 20s or 30s. There is a strong tendency for these worries to run in families and often children learn to worry about ill health from their parents. These preoccupations are usually exacerbated by background stresses and often occur in people who have 'perfectionist' personalities.

Ways of overcoming somatic worries

❶ Understand and accept the psychological processes involved. It is not either physical or psychological but a combination of both.

❷ Stop trying to prove there is nothing wrong with you. We all have to live with uncertainty.

❸ Learn to not ask for reassurance as this makes it worse. Learn to reassure yourself.

❹ Challenge your worrying thoughts. Identify distorted thinking such as 'all or nothing thinking', 'catastrophising or awfulising', jumping to conclusions.

❺ List positive self statements. Draw up a list of five positive self statements on a card and rehearse those statements when feeling preoccupied.

❻ Stop monitoring and checking your symptoms. Distract yourself. Draw up a list of distracting activities that you can engage in.

❼ Stop avoiding things to do with illness, such as hospitals or television programmes, and learn to master your anxiety.

❽ Stop behaving as if you are ill – carry on as normal and keep active.

❾ Stop finding out about illness and reading medical textbooks. Throw away your books.

❿ Reduce your background stress levels. Learn to relax more and build in more pleasurable activities into your life.

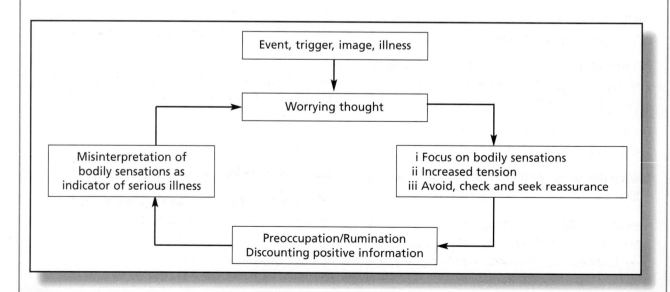

P

Accidents happen all the time, but a trauma is something that 'pierces or wounds our psychological defences'. People might say, 'it really got through to me'. Events that create trauma might range from witnessing an armed robbery, being involved in an assault, a road traffic accident, experiencing physical or sexual abuse, or other disasters. People can experience trauma by being directly or indirectly involved.

Traumas do not occur in isolation, but normally when the person already has an existing agenda of stress to deal with. They also have the habit of triggering past traumatic, frozen memories, which adds further stress and makes the situation worse.

A trauma is something that has challenged a basic fundamental belief that a person holds. The greater the contradiction between what has happened and the belief, the more likely the trauma. If the person strongly believes for example that the world is an orderly, predictable and safe place, or that life is meaningful, or that he or she is a strong, competent person, and this belief is challenged by a catastrophic event, then traumatic stress is likely to ensue.

Normal reactions to trauma

Tearful: Tired and lack of energy . . . poor concentration and memory . . . sleeping difficulties . . . numbness and loss of feeling . . . irritability and lowered tolerance . . . increased muscle tension and arousal . . . nightmares and flashbacks . . . loss of interest . . . headaches . . .

Fear: of similar events happening again, of breaking down or losing control, of being alone, of damage to oneself and loved ones.

Guilt: for surviving or being better of than others, regrets for things not done.

Shame: for not having acted as you would have wished, for having been exposed as helpless, emotional and needy.

Anger: at what happened or who caused it or at the lack of understanding in others.

Disappointed: for all the plans that can never be fulfilled.

Strained relationships: the good feelings may be replaced by conflict, you may not have as much to give, others may not understand or give you what you want.

Ways of coping

❶ **Accept feelings of numbness:** your mind allows the misfortune to be felt only slowly.

❷ **Keep active:** helping others may give some relief, however overactivity is often detrimental if it is a way of not thinking about the event – maintain a balance.

❸ **Confront reality:** confront the reality, attend funerals, return to the scene of the event.

❹ **Seek support:** share with others, allow others to offer physical and emotional support.

❺ **Maintain privacy:** in order to deal with feelings you will find it necessary, at times, to be alone, or just with family and close friends.

❻ **Process your feelings:** it helps to **think, talk and dream** about it over and over again. The more you can do this the better the processing and the quicker you can move forward with your life.

❼ **Understand the meaning of the trauma:** Discuss how it might link up with earlier events in your life.

❽ **Examine and alter unhelpful thinking attributions:** eg, 'I should have done more'.

Some DO'S and DON'TS

DO express your emotions – cry if possible.

DO take every opportunity to review the experience with yourself and others.

DO take time out to sleep, rest, think and be with those important to you.

DO try to keep your life as normal as possible, let children keep up with their activities and stay at school.

DO try to go along with situations or triggers that bring back painful memories of the event, rather than avoiding.

DON'T bottle up feelings.

DON'T avoid talking about what happened.

DON'T expect the memories to go away – the feelings will stay for a long time to come.

Could you describe what effect your complaints have had in the following areas. Please circle the appropriate number.

Effect on Life Inventory

WORK
Because of my problems my work is impaired:

0	1	2	3	4	5	6	7	8
Not at all		Slightly		Significantly		Severely		Very severely

HOME MANAGEMENT
(cleaning, tidying, shopping, cooking, etc)
Because of my problems my home management is impaired:

0	1	2	3	4	5	6	7	8
Not at all		Slightly		Significantly		Severely		Very severely

SOCIAL LEISURE ACTIVITIES
(with other people, eg. parties, pubs, visits, etc)
Because of my problems my social leisure is impaired:

0	1	2	3	4	5	6	7	8
Not at all		Slightly		Significantly		Severely		Very severely

PRIVATE LEISURE ACTIVITIES
(alone, eg, reading, gardening, sewing)
Because of my problems my private leisure is impaired:

0	1	2	3	4	5	6	7	8
Not at all		Slightly		Significantly		Severely		Very severely

FAMILY LIFE
(relations with parents, brothers and sisters, playing with children, etc)
Because of my problems my family life is impaired:

0	1	2	3	4	5	6	7	8
Not at all		Slightly		Significantly		Severely		Very severely

INTIMATE RELATIONSHIPS
(giving affection, hugging, sexual interest, etc)
Because of my problems my intimate relationships are impaired:

0	1	2	3	4	5	6	7	8
Not at all		Slightly		Significantly		Severely		Very severely

P

Please indicate how you are feeling now, or how you have been feeling in the last day or two, by ticking the column to the right of each of the following statements:

	YES DEFINITELY	YES SOMETIMES	NO, NOT MUCH	NO, NOT AT ALL
1 I wake early and then sleep badly for the rest of the night.				
2 I get very frightened or have panic feelings for apparently no reason at all.				
3 I feel miserable and sad.				
4 I feel anxious when I go out of the house on my own.				
5 I have lost interest in things.				
6 I get palpitations, or a sensation of 'butterflies' in my stomach or chest.				
7 I have a good appetite.				
8 I feel scared or frightened.				
9 I feel life is not worth living.				
10 I still enjoy the things I used to.				
11 I am restless and can't keep still.				
12 I am more irritable than usual.				
13 I feel as if I have slowed down.				
14 Worrying thoughts constantly go through my mind.				

Hospital Anxiety & Depression Scale

For scorer's use only:

Anxiety (2, 4, 6, 8, 11, 12, 14) [ ] **A**

Depression (1, 3, 5, 7, 9, 10, 13) [ ] **D**

(Scoring 3, 2, 1, 0)

For scoring items 7 & 10 are reversed

(Suggested cut off point is 8–10 on each scale)

(After **AS Zigmond & RP Snaith**, *Acta Psychiatrica Scandinavica* 67, pp 361–70, Munksgaard International Publishers Ltd, Copenhagen, 1983.)

Please tick the appropriate choice as to how often you have experienced the following physical symptoms during the last two weeks.

Physical Symptoms Inventory

	NOT AT ALL	OCCASIONALLY	OFTEN	MOST OF THE TIME
1 Palpitations				
2 Breathlessness/rapid breathing				
3 Chest pains or discomfort				
4 Choking or smothering sensation				
5 Dizziness or feeling unsteady				
6 Tingling or numbness				
7 Hot and/or cold flushes				
8 Sweating				
9 Fainting				
10 Trembling or shaking				
11 Feeling sick				
12 Upset stomach/diarrhoea				
13 Headaches/migraine				
14 Dry mouth: difficulty swallowing				
15 Feeling of unreality				
16 Tension in jaw/neck/shoulders				
17 Jelly legs				
18 Any other physical symptoms				

P

This section deals with your thoughts and worries about your anxiety. Please tick the appropriate choice as to how often you have experienced the following thoughts during the last two weeks.

	NOT AT ALL	OCCASIONALLY	OFTEN	MOST OF THE TIME
1 I'm going to have a heart attack.				
2 I'm going to faint.				
3 I'm going to look a fool.				
4 Things are getting worse and worse.				
5 People are looking at me.				
6 I'm going to go mad.				
7 I'm going to be too anxious to speak properly.				
8 I'm not going to be able to cope.				
9 I'm going to have a panic attack.				
10 There is something physically wrong with me. I'm ill.				
11 Why do other people cope better than I do?				
12 I can't face up to this because I will not be able to do it.				
13 I'm under a great deal of stress at the moment.				
14 Any other worrying thoughts.				

Worrying Thought Questionnaire

Choose a number from the scale below to show how much you would avoid each of the situations listed below because of fear or other unpleasant feelings. Then write the number you choose in the space opposite each situation.

0	1	2	3	4	5	6	7	8
Would not avoid it	Slightly avoid it			Definitely avoid it		Markedly avoid it		Always avoid it

1	Injections or minor surgery	
2	Eating or drinking with other people	
3	Hospitals	
4	Travelling alone by bus or coach	
5	Walking alone in busy streets	
6	Being watched or stared at	
7	Going into crowded shops	
8	Talking to people in authority	
9	Sight of blood	
10	Being criticised	
11	Going alone far from home	
12	Thought of injury or illness	
13	Speaking or acting to an audience	
14	Large open spaces	
15	Going to the dentist	
16	Other situations (describe)	

Agoraphobia 4, 5, 7 11, 14
Blood & Injury 1, 3, 9, 12, 15
Social 2, 6, 8, 10, 13

Total

(A measure of behavioural avoidance; devised by **I Marks & A Matthews,** 'A brief standardised self-rating scale for phobic patients, *Behaviour Research and Therapy* 17, pp 263–7, 1979.)

P

SECTION 2 – ASSERTIVENESS TRAINING

ASSERTIVENESS TRAINING

■ Books for Professionals and Clients

Alberti R & Emmons M, *Your Perfect Right,* Impact, San Luis Obispo, California, 1974.

Back K & Back K, *Assertiveness at Work – A Practical Guide to Handling Awkward Situations*, McGraw Hill, London, 1982.

Bolton R, *People Skills – How to Assert Yourself, Listen to Others and Resolve Conflict*, Prentice Hall, London, 1986.

Cohen-Posey K, *How to Handle Bullies, Teasers and Other Meanies*, Rainbow Books, New York, 1995.

Covey S, *The Seven Habits of Highly Effective People*, Simon & Schuster, London, 1989.

Dickson A, *A Woman in Your Own Right*, Quartet Books, London, 1982.

Fennell M, *Overcoming Low Self-Esteem*, Robinson, London, 1999.

Goldhor-Lerner H, *The Dance of Anger*, Pandora Press, London, 1992.

Graham RS & Rees S, *Assertiveness Training*, Routledge, London, 1991.

Holland S & Ward C, *Assertiveness: A Practical Approach*, Winslow Press, Bicester, 1990.

Lindenfield G, *Assert Yourself*, Thorson Publishing, Wellingborough, 1986.

Phelps S & Austin N, *The Assertive Woman*, Impact, San Luis Obispo, California, 1975.

Priestly P, McGuire J, Flegg D, Hemsley V & Welham D, *Social Skills and Personal Problem Solving*, Tavistock, London, 1978.

Smith M, *When I Say No I Feel Guilty*, Dial, New York, 1975.

References

**'If you haven't the strength to impose your own terms upon life,
you must accept the terms it offers you'
– T S Eliot –**

What is assertiveness?

The word *assertiveness* is used to describe a certain pattern of behaviour or a style of communicating with others. It is a way of behaving which means we are communicating our feelings, thoughts and beliefs in an open, honest manner without violating the rights of other people. It is an alternative to being either aggressive, where we abuse other people's rights, or to being passive, where we abuse our own rights.

Being assertive means we are able to ask for what we want from others; it means we can say 'no' to the requests of others; it means we can express a range and depth of emotion, for example, love, liking and anger; and it means we can express personal opinions without feeling self-conscious. Very few people manage to be assertive all the time in all areas of their lives. It is undoubtedly true that we could all benefit from being more assertive in some areas of our lives.

Why are we unassertive?

We act in an unassertive manner because we have learned through our experiences to behave that way. This learning process can be traced back to our early childhood. Small babies have no fear of expressing themselves and communicating their needs. They cry and smile openly; there is no inhibition or 'beating about the bush'. But very quickly children learn to adapt their behaviour to the kind of responses they receive from those around them. Children's behaviour is subtly shaped by the models they are exposed to and by the encouragement, or lack of it, received from parents, family, friends and school.

Some children are encouraged and rewarded for expressing themselves openly and honestly and are quite comfortable expressing a range of emotions. Others may be encouraged to express their thoughts but find it more difficult to express emotions. We have all learned to be the way we are; therefore we can learn to behave differently.

The effects of being unassertive

The long-term effect of being unassertive is a growing loss of *self-esteem*. This term refers to our own evaluation of ourselves in respect to how competent, significant and likeable we see ourselves as people. The more we act in an unassertive way, the weaker is our positive sense of identity: the sense of, 'this is me, this is how I feel and how I think'. This can result in a lack of sense of purpose, or a feeling that we are not in control of our lives, which in turn leads to negative feelings and symptoms of stress.

If we are failing to express ourselves openly and we are concealing our feelings and thoughts, this can lead to internal tension, also resulting in physical and mental symptoms of stress. Inherent in unassertive behaviour is poor communication which leads to the development of unhealthy uncomfortable relationships. Communicating effectively in relationships is the best possible insulator against symptoms of stress, anxiety and depression.

Why be more assertive?

By being more assertive we can improve our sense of identity, our confidence and our self-esteem. A snowball effect is created: the more confident we feel, the more assertive we are and so on. By stating more clearly what our needs are, we increase the chances that these needs will be met.

Being assertive leads to a saving in energy and a reduction in tension. We are no longer preoccupied with avoiding upsetting others, and no longer overly concerned with making gains in an aggressive way. People who are generally assertive are confident people who are simply happy to be themselves.

'God give me the strength to change that which I need to
change, the patience to accept that which I cannot
change, and above all, the wisdom to know the difference'

– The Serenity Prayer –

Steps in the Programme

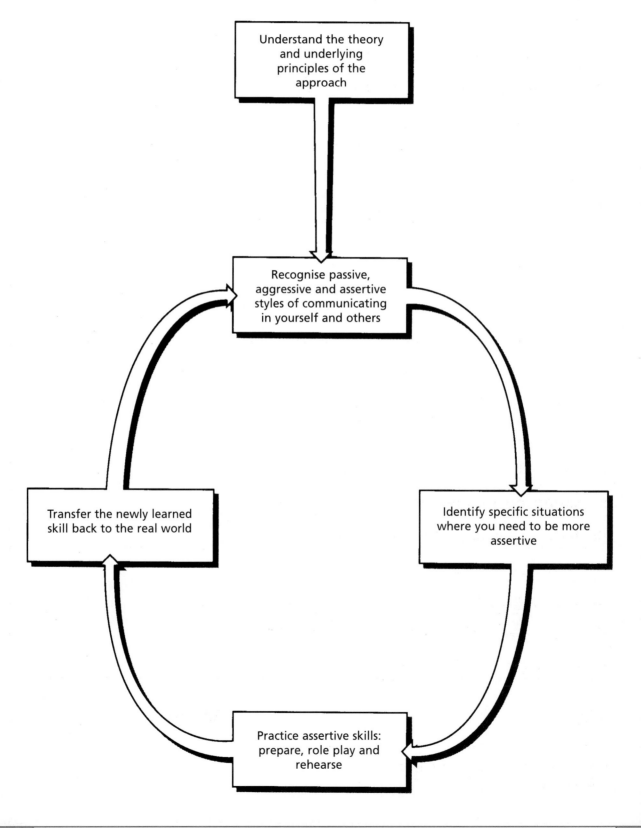

Understand the theory and underlying principles of the approach

Recognise passive, aggressive and assertive styles of communicating in yourself and others

Identify specific situations where you need to be more assertive

Transfer the newly learned skill back to the real world

Practice assertive skills: prepare, role play and rehearse

P

Indicate how comfortable you feel in each of the following situations.

Score **1** if you feel very uncomfortable
  2 if you feel slightly uncomfortable
  3 if you feel reasonably comfortable
  4 if you feel very comfortable.

		ENTER 1, 2, 3 or 4
1	Asking for the service you expect when you haven't received it in a shop or restaurant	
2	Expressing anger when you are angry	
3	Receiving a compliment and saying something to acknowledge that you agree	
4	Discussing another person's criticism of you openly with them	
5	Speaking up in front of a group	
6	Telling a friend that they are doing something that bothers you	
7	Requesting the return of a borrowed item without apology	
8	Initiating a conversation with a stranger	
9	Telling an acquaintance that you like him or her	
10	Returning a defective item to a shop or restaurant	
11	Asking a favour of someone	
12	Turning down a request for a meeting or date	
13	Admitting to either fear or ignorance	
14	Asking for and accepting constructive criticism	
15	Saying 'no' to someone without being apologetic	
16	Telling a friend exactly how you feel	
17	Arguing with another person	
18	Touching a colleague or friend affectionately	
19	Treating yourself or doing something just for you	
20	Refusing a friend a favour when you don't want to do it	

Scoring   Total Score

Over 55   You are assertive
40–55   You could be more assertive
Under 40 You are unassertive

At times we can all become prone to negative, irrational thinking which causes a block to assertive behaviour. We need to identify these negative thoughts, or obstacles, and then to challenge them. Are they based on irrational beliefs? Examine the following list, and note which of the thoughts and styles of faulty thinking you are most prone to:

1   *It is uncaring, rude, and selfish to say what you want.*

2   *If I assert myself I will upset the other person and ruin our relationship.*

3   *It will be terribly embarrassing if I say what I think.*

4   *If someone says 'no' to my request it is because they don't like or love me.*

5   *I shouldn't have to say what I need or how I feel; people close to me should already know.*

6   *I have no right to change my mind; neither has anybody else.*

7   *I don't really mind the present situation.*

8   *It will all work out in the end, and anyway, it's not my fault.*

9   *People should keep their feelings to themselves.*

10   *I shouldn't say how I'm really feeling or thinking because I don't want to burden others with my problems.*

Add any other negative thoughts you can think of.

P

'Man is born to live and not to prepare to live'

– Boris Pasternak –

The underlying philosophy of assertiveness training is based on the premise that we are all equal and that we all possess the same basic rights. Many people seem to have forgotten, or have never been told, that these rights exist. The goal of assertiveness is to stand up for your rights without violating the rights of others. A good starting point is to remind yourself of some of these basic rights.

1   *I have the right to express my feelings.*

2   *I have the right to express my opinions and beliefs.*

3   *I have the right to say 'yes' and 'no' for myself.*

4   *I have the right to change my mind.*

5   *I have the right to say, 'I don't understand'.*

6   *I have the right simply to be myself without having to act for other people's benefit.*

7   *I have the right to decline responsibility for other people's problems.*

8   *I have the right to make reasonable requests of others.*

9   *I have the right to set my own priorities.*

10   *I have the right to be listened to, and taken seriously.*

11   *I have the right to make mistakes and feel comfortable about admitting to them.*

12   *I have the right to be illogical in making decisions.*

13   *I have the right to say, 'I don't care'.*

14   *I have the right to be miserable or cheerful.*

Add any other rights that you can think of.

Definition

This involves violating your own rights by failing to express honest feelings, thoughts and beliefs, and consequently permitting others to violate your rights. Passive or non-assertive behaviour can also mean expressing your thoughts and feelings in such an apologetic and self-effacing manner that others can easily disregard them. The passive responder allows others to walk all over them, like a doormat. Non-assertive people feel they have no control over events: they are controlled and immobilised. Passive people do not allow their needs to take precedence over, or be as valid as, others. They allow others to make their decisions for them, even though they may resent it later. They feel helpless, powerless and inhibited. Non-assertion sometimes shows a subtle lack of respect for the other person's ability to take disappointments, to shoulder some responsibility, and to handle their own problems.

The person who behaves passively is occasionally prone to such a build up of stress and anger that they eventually explode in a really aggressive manner.

Message communicated

I don't count, so you can take advantage of me. My feelings, needs and thoughts are less important than yours. I'll put up with just about anything from you.

Subconscious thoughts

Take care of me and understand my needs telepathically. Will you still love/respect me if I am assertive? I've got to protect you from hurt.

Goal

To appease others and to avoid conflict and unpleasantness at any cost.

Verbal and non-verbal characteristics

◆ Rambling; letting things slide without comment

◆ Beating about the bush – not saying what you mean

◆ Apologising inappropriately in a soft, unsteady voice

◆ Being unclear; averting gaze

◆ Posture – backing off from others, slouching shoulders

◆ Wringing hands; winking or laughing when expressing anger

◆ Covering mouth with hand

◆ Using phrases such as, '. . . if it wouldn't be too much trouble', '. . . but do whatever you want', 'I . . . er . . . um . . . would like . . . um . . . you . . . er . . . to do . . .'

Payoffs

You are praised for being selfless, a good sport. If things go wrong, as a passive follower, you are rarely blamed. Others will protect and look after you. You avoid, postpone, or hide the conflict that you fear.

Price

Others often make unreasonable demands on you. When, by your lack of assertion, you have allowed a relationship to develop in a way you don't like, then shifting the pattern becomes more difficult. You restrict yourself into other people's images of a lovable, good person. When you repress or bottle up so much anger and frustration, you simultaneously diminish other more positive feelings in yourself, including love and affection.

P

■ Definition

This involves standing up for your personal rights and expressing your thoughts, feelings and beliefs in a way which is usually inappropriate and always violates the rights of the other person. People often feel devastated by an encounter with an aggressive person. Superiority is maintained by putting others down. When threatened, you attack, aiming at the vulnerability exposed in the other.

■ Message communicated

This is what I think, what I want, what I feel. What matters to you isn't important to me.

■ Subconscious thoughts

I'll get you, before you have a chance of getting me. I'm out for Number One. The world is a battle ground and I am out to win.

■ Goal

To dominate, to win, to force the other person to lose, and to punish.

■ Verbal and non-verbal characteristics

◆ Intruding into the other's space

◆ Staring the other person out

◆ Strident, sarcastic or condescending voice

◆ Parental body gestures (eg, finger pointing)

◆ Threats (eg, 'You'd better watch out . . .', 'If you don't . . .')

◆ Put downs (eg, 'You've got to be kidding', 'Don't be so stupid')

◆ Evaluative comments (ie, emphasising concepts like 'should', 'bad', 'ought')

◆ Sexist/racist remarks

■ Payoffs

You get others to do your bidding. Things tend to go your way and you like that feeling of control in shaping your life. You are likely to secure the material needs and objects you desire. You are less vulnerable in a culture characterised by struggle, hostility and competition.

■ Price

Aggressive behaviour creates enemies, which can induce greater fear and a sense of paranoia, making life more difficult for you. If, through your aggression, you control what others do, this takes time and mental energy and makes it difficult for you to relax. Relationships tend to be based on negative emotions and are likely to be unstable.

Aggressive people often do feel inferior deep down and try to compensate for that by putting others down.

Definition

This involves standing up for your personal rights and expressing your thoughts, feelings and beliefs directly, honestly and openly in ways that are respectful of the rights of others. An assertive person acts without undue anxiety or guilt. Assertive people respect themselves and other people and take responsibility for their actions and choices. They recognise their needs and ask openly and directly for what they want. If refused, they may feel saddened, disappointed or inconvenienced, but their self-concept isn't shattered. They are not over-reliant on the approval of others, and feel secure and confident within themselves. Assertive people give the lead to other people as to how they wish to be treated.

Message communicated

This is what I think. This is how I feel. This is how I see the situation. How about you? If our needs conflict, I am certainly ready to explore our differences and I may be prepared to compromise.

Subconscious thoughts

I won't allow you to take advantage of me and I won't attack you for being who you are.

Goal

To communicate clearly, adult to adult.

Verbal and non-verbal characteristics

◆ Receptive listening

◆ Firm, relaxed voice

◆ Direct eye contact

◆ Erect, balanced, open body stance

◆ Voice appropriately loud for the situation

◆ 'I' statements ('I like', 'I want', 'I don't like')

◆ Cooperative phrases ('What are your thoughts on this?')

◆ Emphatic statements of interest ('I would like to. . .')

Payoffs

The more you stand up for yourself and act in a manner you respect, the higher your self-esteem. Your chances of getting what you want out of life improve greatly when you let others know what you want and stand up for your own rights and needs. Expressing yourself directly at the time of negative feelings means that resentment is not allowed to build up. Being less preoccupied with self-consciousness and anxiety, and less driven by the needs of self-protection and control, you can see, hear and love others more easily.

Price

Friends may have benefited from your non-assertion and may sabotage your newly developed assertion. You are reshaping your beliefs and re-examining values that have been closely held since childhood. This can be frightening. There are no 'tablets of stone' to guarantee an elegant outcome of your efforts. There is often pain involved in being assertive.

Rate each response in terms of being either passive, assertive or aggressive by ticking the appropriate column.

	Passive	Assertive	Aggressive
1 In a no-smoking compartment of a crowded train a fellow passenger lights a cigarette. Julie hates the smell of cigarettes.			
RESPONSE A Julie gets up and leaves the compartment.			
RESPONSE B Julie starts coughing and spluttering then says to the man, 'Listen, that is a disgusting, antisocial habit. I don't care if you kill yourself, but I don't want to die. Put that cigarette out or go to another compartment.'			
RESPONSE C Julie points to the 'No Smoking' sign and says, 'This is a non-smoking compartment. Would you mind moving to a smoking area as I really don't like the smoke.'			
2 In a packed cinema the people behind Mr Brown keep talking in a fairly loud voice, detracting from his enjoyment of the film. The cinema is so crowded that he can't change seats.			
RESPONSE A Mr Brown suffers in silence and says nothing.			
RESPONSE B Mr Brown turns around and snarls at them, 'Don't you have any respect for others? If you don't shut up immediately I'll call the manager and have you thrown out.'			
RESPONSE C Mr Brown turns around, looks directly at the talkers and says, 'Your talking is distracting me from the film.'			
3 Mary, a secretary, is given a large piece of typing to complete at five minutes to five. She is planning to go out that evening and wants to leave at five o'clock.			
RESPONSE A Mary is really angry and thinks, 'What a thoughtless boss I have. I told him I was going out tonight.' She suffers in silence and leaves work at 6.15 feeling angry and irritable.			
RESPONSE B Mary explains to her boss that she'd like to leave on time and that she would do the work first thing next morning unless it was really very urgent.			
RESPONSE C Mary feels angry but starts the work. At about 5.30 she explodes, kicks the waste paper bin and storms into her boss's office saying that she's sick of the job and his thoughtlessness. She goes home and feels guilty for her anger.			

Identifying Response Styles

Everyday situations that may require assertiveness

AT WORK

How do you respond when:

❶ You receive a compliment on your appearance, or someone praises your work?

❷ You are criticised unfairly?

❸ You are criticised legitimately by a superior?

❹ You have to confront a subordinate for continual lateness or sloppy work?

❺ Your boss makes a sexual innuendo, or makes a pass at you?

AT HOME

How do you respond when:

❶ One of your parents criticises you?

❷ You are irritated by a persistent habit in someone you love?

❸ Everybody leaves the washing-up to you?

❹ You want to say 'No' to a proposed visit to a relative?

❺ Your partner feels amorous but you are not in the mood?

IN PUBLIC

How do you respond when:

❶ In a restaurant the food you ordered arrives cold or overcooked?

❷ A fellow passenger in a non-smoking compartment lights a cigarette?

❸ You are faced with an unhelpful shop assistant?

❹ Somebody barges in front of you in a queue?

❺ You take an inferior article back to a shop?

AMONGST FRIENDS

How do you respond when:

❶ You feel angry with the way a friend has treated you?

❷ A friend makes what you consider to be an unreasonable request?

❸ You want to ask a friend for a favour?

❹ You ask a friend for repayment of a loan of money?

❺ You have to negotiate with a friend on which film to see or where to meet?

P

'Discontent is the first step in progress'

– Chinese proverb –

Write down 10 situations from any area of your life in which you would like to be more assertive (home, work, public, friends).

When you have the list in front of you, write down next to each situation how you behave now (passive, aggressive, both). You may find you need to write down more than one category if you respond differently at different times.

Look at the list and see if you can arrange it in order of difficulty. Find the situation which you can almost handle assertively but not quite and number it 1 – the most difficult situation will be numbered 10.

EXAMPLE LIST

1 Ask the lodger to put top on toothpaste. (*Passive*)
2 Ask children to tidy up their bedrooms. (*Aggressive*)
3 Ask my sister to return the cassette recorder that she borrowed. (*Passive*)
4 Tell neighbours to keep noise down at night (*Passive/aggressive*)
5 Tell wife when I feel I want to be left alone. (*Aggressive*)
6 Tell Mum how much I like her and give her a cuddle. (*Passive*)
7 Tell my mother-in-law that I do not want her to smoke cigarettes in my house. (*Passive*)
8 Apologise to a colleague for snapping at her the other day. (*Passive*)
9 Delegate teaching commitments to a colleague for next six months. (*Passive*)
10 Ring the bank manager and tell him I need more time to make up my mind. (*Passive*)

YOUR LIST

1
2
3
4
5
6
7
8
9
10

Order of difficulty: 1 Easiest ⟶ 10 Most difficult.

'To feel brave, act as if you were brave'

– William James –

The following is a list of behaviour assignments or homework exercises which will prove useful in increasing your level of assertiveness. Choose an assignment which would be moderately difficult and set a deadline to do it. If you haven't done it by that time, either assume it was too difficult and choose another task, or alternatively, introduce a reward or incentive for doing it by another specified time.

1   *Say 'good morning' to somebody to whom you do not usually speak.*

2   *Stop two people in the street and ask for directions.*

3   *Go into an expensive shop, try on a number of articles of clothing, but buy nothing.*

4   *Go into a shop and ask if they will give you change for a five pound note.*

5   *Pay a compliment to a waitress, shop assistant or fellow-worker.*

6   *Without expecting a response, make a comment to the person next to you in a queue, or on a bus.*

7   *Buy something from a shop and then deliberately return it, saying, 'I've changed my mind'.*

8   *Deliberately touch someone you like on the arm or shoulder.*

9   *Tell your spouse or close friend something personal about yourself that you have never told anybody before.*

10   *Make a point of telling a joke or a funny story to a friend.*

11   *Ask somebody you know, 'How are you today?' and deliberately take an interest; try to draw them out and find out how they are feeling.*

12   *Make a point of telling somebody how you are feeling, and/or what you have being doing recently.*

13   *Tell somebody that you like something about their appearance, for example, 'I like that tie'.*

14   *Tell somebody close to you something that has been irritating you about them which you haven't ever mentioned before.*

15   *Ask someone for a favour in a direct way.*

P

Practice Exercises for Assertion

Directions: *Fill in each block with a rating of your assertiveness on a 5-point scale.*
A rating of 0 means you have no difficulty asserting yourself.
A rating of 5 means you are completely unable to assert yourself.

PEOPLE / ACTIVITY	Service workers, waiters, shop assistants	Strangers	Colleagues and subordinates	Relatives, family members	Authority figures	Intimate relations or spouse	Friends of different sex	Friends of the same sex
Giving compliments								
Making requests, eg, ask for favours/help								
Initiating and maintaining conversation								
Refusing requests								
Expressing personal opinions								
Expressing anger/displeasure								
Expressing like, love, affection								
Stating your rights and needs								

Being a good listener is an important skill in any relationship, whether at work or at home. Therapists, counsellors and interviewers learn and practice these skills of attending, following and reflecting. Examine these skills and practice the ones that you are poorest at.

■ Attending skills

A posture of involvement
Incline your body towards speaker – facing squarely – open posture – appropriate distance.

Appropriate body motion
Moving in a synchronised way with the speaker, not to distract, not rigid and unmoving.

Eye contact
With face and other parts of body – not staring, not avoiding.

Non-distracting environment
No distractors – remove sizeable physical barriers.

■ Following skills

Door openers
Non-coercive invitations to talk – a description of the other person's body language – 'Care to talk about it?' Silence – attending.

Minimal encouragers
'Mm-hmmm . . . really . . . right . . . oh!', head nodding.

Infrequent questions
Open questions, eg, 'How did that make you feel?', rather than, 'Do you like him?'; ask only one question at a time.

Attentive silence
Offers personal space to think, feel and express.

■ Reflecting skills

Paraphrasing
A concise response stating the essence of the other's content in the listener's own words.

Reflecting feelings
Mirroring back to the speaker, in succinct statements, the emotions they are communicating – focus on feeling words – observe body language. Ask yourself how you would feel in that situation. 'You look pretty upset.' 'Sounds like you're really angry.'

Reflecting meaning
Linking the speaker's feelings to facts to provide meaning. 'You feel angry because of "a", "b" and "c" . . .'

Summarising
Brief restatement of the main themes and feelings the speaker expressed over a long conversation.

(Adapted from **Bolton,** 1986)

 P

Some people tend to spoil good communication in a number of ways: by judging the other person; by always sending a solution; or by avoiding the other's emotional concerns. These behaviours get in the way of good quality expressive communication and relationships.

■ Judging

Criticising
Making a negative evaluation of the other person, 'You brought it on yourself . . .'

Name calling
Putting down or stereotyping the other person, 'You are just another insensitive male'.

Diagnosing
Playing emotional detective – analysing, 'Just because you went to college'.

Praising evaluatively
Over-praising, or manipulating by praise, can produce a defensive response, 'You're such a good girl, will you . . .'

■ Sending solutions

Ordering
A solution sent coercively can produce resistance, resentment and sabotage, especially when backed by force, 'will you talk to me'.

Threatening
A solution sent with an emphasis on punishment, 'Do it or else I'm leaving', produces the same results as ordering.

Moralising
Telling another person what they should or ought to do – it is demoralising and fosters anxiety and resentment.

Excessive/inappropriate questioning
Closed-ended questions can be real conversation stoppers, answered in a few words, 'Are you tired now?' (closed). 'How are you feeling now?' (open).

Advising
Giving a solution to their problems implies a lack of confidence in the other person's ability to understand and to cope. 'If I was you I would . . .', sometimes the person may not want advice but may want to be listened to.

■ Avoiding the other's concerns

Diverting
Pushing the other's problem aside through distraction. 'Don't dwell on it, let's talk about something else.' A form of emotional withdrawal.

Logical argument
When another person is under stress or very emotional, an appeal to logic without consideration of the emotions can be infuriating, and a way of avoiding emotional involvement.

Reassuring
Trying to stop the other person from feeling the negative emotions he or she is experiencing, 'Don't worry, everything will work out in the end.' It can be a form of emotional withdrawal.

Adapted from **Bolton** (1986).

Common Communication Spoilers

Non-Verbal Behaviour

	PASSIVE	ASSERTIVE	AGGRESSIVE
Body movements	◆ Hand wringing ◆ Hunching shoulders ◆ Covering mouth with hands ◆ Crossing arms for protection	◆ Open hand movements ◆ Sitting/standing upright and relaxed	◆ Finger pointing ◆ Fist clenching ◆ Striding around (impatiently) ◆ Leaning forward or over ◆ Crossing arms (unapproachable)
Eye contact	◆ Evasive ◆ Looking down	◆ Firm direct eye contact without staring	◆ Trying to stare down and intimidate
Facial expression	◆ 'Ghost' smiles when expressing anger or being criticised ◆ Raising eyebrows in anticipation ◆ Jaw trembling, lip biting ◆ Quick-changing features	◆ Smiling when pleased ◆ Frowning when angry ◆ Features steady ◆ Jaw relaxed	◆ Smiling may become sneering ◆ Scowling when angry ◆ Jaws set firm
Speech pattern	◆ Hesitant and filled with pauses ◆ Sometimes jerking from fast to slow ◆ Frequent throat clearing	◆ Fluent, few hesitations ◆ Emphasising key words ◆ Steady even pace	◆ Fluent, few hesitations ◆ Often abrupt, clipped ◆ Emphasising blaming words ◆ Often fast
Voice	◆ Often dull and monotonous ◆ Tone may be singsong or whining ◆ Over-soft or over-warm ◆ Quiet, often dropping away	◆ Steady and firm ◆ Tone is middle range, rich and warm ◆ Sincere and clear ◆ Not over-loud or quiet	◆ Very firm ◆ Tone is sarcastic, sometimes cold and harsh ◆ Hard and sharp ◆ Strident, often shouting, rising at end

P

TYPE OF LANGUAGE		
PASSIVE	**ASSERTIVE**	**AGGRESSIVE**
Long rambling statements	**'I' statements that are brief, clear and to the point**	**Excessive emphasis on 'I'** 'My view is . . .', 'I think'
Fill in words 'Maybe', 'Er', 'Sort of'	'I like', 'I feel', 'I think', 'I prefer'	**Boastfulness** 'I haven't got problems like you'
Frequent justifications 'I wouldn't normally say anything, only . . .'	**Distinction between fact and opinion** 'My experience is different'.	**Opinion expressed as fact** 'That's a useless way to do it', 'Nobody wants to behave like that'
Apologies 'I'm terribly sorry to bother you . . .', 'Please excuse me, but . . .'	**Suggestions without 'shoulds', 'oughts'.** 'How about', 'Would you like me to . . .?'	**Threatening questions** 'Haven't you finished it yet?' 'Why on earth did you do it like that?'
Unacknowledged choice 'I should', 'I ought', 'I have to'	**Constructive criticism without blame** 'I feel irritated when you interrupt me'	**Threatening requests** 'You'd better do that', 'I want that done or else'
Qualifiers 'It's only my opinion', 'I might be wrong'	**Seeking other's opinions** 'How does this fit in with your ideas?'	**Heavy handed advice** 'You should', 'You ought', 'Why don't you?'
Self-dismissal 'It's not important', 'It really doesn't matter'	**Willingness to explore other solutions** 'How can we get around this problem?'	**Blame** 'You made a mess of that'
Self-putdowns 'I'm useless . . . hopeless', 'You know me'		**Sarcasm** 'You must be joking', 'I don't suppose you managed to do that?'

1 Being specific

Decide what it is you want or feel, and say so specifically or directly. This skill will help you to be clear about what exactly it is you want to communicate. Avoid unnecessary padding and keep your statement simple and brief.

2 Repetition (broken record technique)

This skill involves preparing what you are going to say and repeating it exactly, as often as necessary, in a calm relaxed manner. It helps you to stick to your statement or request without being distracted. Using this technique, you can relax because you know what you are going to say and you can maintain a steady comment, avoiding irrelevant logic or argumentative bait.

3 Workable compromise

This is important to remember when there is a conflict between your needs or wishes, and those of someone else. Assertiveness is not about winning, so you need to negotiate from an equal position. This means finding a true compromise which takes both parties' needs into consideration. Compromising on a solution to a difficult situation need not compromise your self-respect.

4 Self-disclosure

This skill allows you to disclose your feelings with a simple statement, for example, 'I feel nervous' or 'I feel guilty'. The immediate effect is to reduce your anxiety, enabling you to relax and take charge of yourself and your feelings.

5 Negative assertion

This skill involves calmly agreeing with someone else's true criticism of your negative qualities and accepting that you have faults eg, 'Your desk is a complete and utter tip. You are very disorganised.' 'Yes, it's true, I'm not very tidy.' The key to using negative assertion is, of course, self-confidence and a belief that you have the ability to change yourself if you so wish. By agreeing with and accepting criticism, if it is appropriate, you need not feel totally demolished.

6 Negative inquiry

This skill involves actively prompting criticism of your behaviour, to ascertain whether the criticism is constructive, or to expose it as manipulative and hurtful. For example, 'You'll find that difficult won't you, because you are so shy?' You reply, 'In what ways do you think I'm shy?' If the criticism is constructive, that information can be used constructively and the general channel of communication will be improved.

 P

Some people find it exceedingly difficult to say no. This often means that they spend a great deal of their time doing things for other people that they really do not want to do. This can often lead to a gradual build-up of resentment and frustration which can poison relationships. It also means that people often feel that they have little control over their time and their life in general. It is rather like feeling flooded and not being able to turn the tap off. Saying 'no' to the demands of others is the equivalent of turning off the tap of external demands or stresses. It puts you in the driver's seat and means that you have more control over your life and time.

■ Beliefs about Saying 'No'

❶ There appear to be a number of key beliefs which would predispose people to have difficulty saying 'no'. These beliefs need to be challenged and modified.

a Saying 'no' is rude and aggressive.
b Saying 'no' is unkind, uncaring and selfish.
c Saying 'no' will hurt and upset others and make them feel rejected.
d If I say 'no' to somebody they will cease to like me.
e Other's needs are more important than mine.
f Saying 'no' over little things is small minded and petty.

❷ The key to refusing requests and saying 'no' is to be able to accept the following belief.

a 'Other people have the right to ask, and I have the right to refuse'.
b 'When you say "no" you are refusing a request, not rejecting a person'.
  We may have come to associate saying 'no' with rejection, but refusal does not have to mean rejection. Refusing the behaviour or request and rejecting the person are two quite different things.
c When we say 'yes' to one thing we are actually saying no to something else. We always have a choice and we are continuously making choices.

❸ People who have difficulty saying 'no' usually over estimate the difficulty that the other

person will have in accepting the refusal. By expressing our feelings openly and honestly, it actually liberates the other person to express their feelings. By saying 'no' to somebody it allows them to say 'no' to your requests while still also being able to ask for further requests.

■ Hints for saying 'no'

❹ a As a rule keep it brief – avoid long rambling justifications.
b Be polite – saying something like, 'thank you for asking . . .'.
c Speak slowly with warmth otherwise 'no' may sound abrupt.
d Be honest about your feelings. It may help to say 'I find this difficult'.

■ Ways of saying 'no'

❺ a *Direct 'no'*. The aim is to say no without apologising. The other person has the problem but you do not have to allow him or her to pass it on to you. A direct no can be quite forceful and can be effective with salespeople.
b *Reflecting 'no'*. This technique involves reflecting back the content and feeling of the request, but adding your assertive refusal at the end. For example; 'I know you're looking forward to a walk this afternoon, but I can't come'.
c *Reasoned 'no'*. This gives, very briefly, the genuine reason for the refusal. For example; 'I can't come for a walk this afternoon because I've got to work on my book'.
d *Raincheck 'no'*. This says 'no' to the present request but leaves room for negotiation. For example; 'I can't come for a walk this afternoon, but I'd like to go this evening'.
e *Enquiring 'no'*. This is not a definite 'no' and again could be a prelude to negotiation. For example; 'Is there any other time you'd like to go?'
f *Broken record 'no'*. This involves repeating a simple statement of refusal over and over again if the requester is very persistent. For example; 'No, I don't want to this afternoon'. 'Oh come on it's a lovely day', 'No I don't want to this afternoon'.

'The man who gets angry at the right things and with the right people, and in the right way, and at the right time, and for the right length of time, is commended'

– Aristotle –

Anger is a normal, healthy human emotion which, if not expressed, can lead to long-term consequences, such as anxiety, depression, irritability and a variety of physical complaints. Anger can sometimes be a creative source of energy that helps us to move forward, and motivates us to change our lives. Some people, particularly women, are from an early age, discouraged from expressing anger and pay a price for being 'too nice'. We may have internalised a number of unhelpful beliefs that need reassessing.

'Getting angry is not the correct way to behave.'

This is an unreal expectation; many children are brought up to believe it is wrong to express anger. So they live with a feeling of failure every time they get angry. In fact, showing appropriate anger can be positive. Genuine grievances can be brought to the notice of others, and problems can then be resolved by discussion.

'Getting angry is destructive and negative.'

People often assume that anger is destructive to a person or to a relationship. In fact, anger can make the other person sit up and take notice. When anger is expressed at the time of the grievance, it then feels less destructive and explosive.

'If I express my anger, it will completely wreck him.'

People are often unwilling to express anger directly, fearing that the other person is too frail to cope with it. In fact, this is very unlikely; they may have communicated frailty in order to manipulate you. Once you have expressed your bottled-up anger, the realities of the relationship will be in the open, therefore more manageable and less explosive.

'If I allow myself to get angry, I might lose control and cause injury.'

Many people believe that the consequences of expressing anger directly will be catastrophic, for example they might explode or injure or even kill the other person. In fact, letting out angry feelings, when appropriate, helps us to become familiar with the feelings, less frightened of them and better able to control them.

'If I get angry, they will get me back in return.'

This belief usually originates in childhood if expressions of anger were strongly punished by parents or other adults. Many of the consequences of expressing anger, feared from childhood, will in reality not happen in adulthood.

'If I get angry, I will be rejected.'

In some more formal relationships, getting angry may lead to a negative response, but in a close relationship, being able to express anger means you are accepted by the other person as you are, not as an ideal.

 P

The assertive person can accept and learn from criticism. It may at times be painful but it is necessary for any self improvement. People who are predominantly passive very often do not hear, or benefit from, constructive criticism. Rather, their reaction is to readily agree with the criticism – 'Yes you're right, I'm hopeless' – and then emotionally drown in a sea of self-reproach. People who are locked into an aggressive communication style are also often impervious to criticism as they tend to see it as a personal attack. Their reaction is 'how dare you', and their response is to fight and defend themselves to prove that they are winners. They do not actually listen or learn from the criticism at all.

How we react to criticism is largely based on our early experience as children. If as a child we experienced criticism as a hurtful rejection we may find it hard to take as adults. If as a child criticism was carried out lovingly it will be easier to accept. Perhaps as a child the person did not experience any criticism at all and therefore as an adult finds it devastating.

It is very important to differentiate between a person's behaviour being criticised, and the person as a whole being criticised. So for example, if we are told, 'You are stupid' – that is negative labelling of the whole person and tends to be experienced as rejecting. However, if we are told 'that was a stupid thing to do' – that is a comment on our behaviour, and implies that we have the power to change that behaviour. There is a big difference.

Coping with Constructive Criticism

❶ **Accept the criticism**

The simplest response to realistic criticism is to accept it without expressing any guilt or other negative emotions. We all have faults, make mistakes. If we can accept this reality we can learn from it. So the response to, 'you are always so untidy', might be, 'Yes, I am sometimes untidy, and I'm trying to be tidier'. Do not be afraid to say, 'sorry, I made a mistake'.

❷ **Ask for information**

This also involves accepting the criticism, if we feel that it is soundly based, but also actually asking for clarification from the person who is criticising us to try and pin down the precise

nature of the criticism. So, the response to, 'You made a mess of that', might be, 'Yes, what was it that was particularly bad?'

Coping with destructive criticism

❶ **Disagree with the criticism:** This involves a straight forward, calm assertive disagreement, 'No, I'm not always late'.

❷ **Ask for information:** This involves asking for more information from your critic to expose whether the criticism is constructive or destructive. If the criticism is constructive the information from the critic will be useful and your relationship will be enriched. If it is destructive the criticiser might be put on the spot. For example, 'In what way do you think that I am hopeless?'

❸ **Fogging:** This skill helps us deal with destructive criticism and put downs designed to make us feel bad. It involves agreeing with anything which is obviously true in the criticism but neither agreeing nor disagreeing with other aspects of the criticism. If, for example, somebody describes you as being dreadfully lazy and untidy, your response might be 'Yes you're probably right, I am sometimes untidy'. By using fogging you merely aim to stop the manipulative criticism, by refusing to reward the put-down. Your attacker wants you to feel bad, and if he or she does not get the sought response eg, a fight, but gets smothered in the 'fog', it is not rewarding and they are less likely try again.

Giving Constructive Criticism

❶ Choose the right time and place.

❷ Stay calm and speak slowly.

❸ Focus on a specific behaviour, avoid sweeping generalisations and other items from the past and avoid undermining the person.

❹ Acknowledge the positive first. Sandwich a negative comment in between two positive comments.

❺ Do not use labels, stereotypes or insults.

The art of negotiation, or resolving grievances, like many assertiveness skills, is becoming a profession in its own right. We certainly do not need sophisticated training to negotiate solutions to everyday problems, but the following points are worth bearing in mind.

❶ Choose the right time and place

Setting time aside to have a joint discussion is preferable to presenting a problem when the other person is busy or preoccupied with other problems.

❷ Present the problem in a constructive way

Work out beforehand the points you want to make and how to put them. Write them down. Be specific, don't beat about the bush as this only causes confusion about the issue you are trying to raise. Be tactful; being sarcastic or unpleasant only results in the other person becoming defensive and resistant to change. Keep calm, if possible using relaxation techniques to help you prepare. At the very least take a couple of long, slow, deep breaths before you start.

❸ Listen to what the other person has got to say

Concentrate on what is being said and let the other person know you understand what he or she is saying. Summarise the other person's position and feed it back: 'So your view is that . . .' If the other person is showing feelings, acknowledge that you are aware of them, for example, 'I can see that this is difficult for you'. Ask for clarification. Make sure that you fully understand the other person's position, reasoning and needs.

❹ Discuss differences

Restate your original case, then present a summary of the other person's position. Discuss the specific areas of difference. Beware of becoming side-tracked; don't fall

for red herrings. Sometimes the broken record technique is useful to bring the discussion back to the central subject (see handout 'Six Assertiveness Skills').

❺ Be prepared to offer a compromise

Remember the issue is not about winning or losing, but about reaching a compromise that is acceptable to both parties. Don't be stubborn and wait for the other person to give in first. Make a concession and look for one in return. Emphasise that you both share a common goal and that you are willing to explore how that can be achieved.

Dealing with personal grievances

a Acknowledge your own feelings to yourself eg, anger, hurt. 'I feel . . .'

b Write down what it is that you do not like. Separate fact from feeling. 'I don't like you doing . . .'

c Identify what you would like. 'I would like it if . . .'

d Arrange a meeting.

e State your grievance. Feelings first, followed by what you would like. Do not get distracted or use critical words. State what you would like.

f Listen to the other person.

g Discuss differences.

h Reach agreements if possible.

 P

Sulking, being unwilling to talk, or withdrawing from engaging in constructive communication, is an unhelpful way of communicating either anger or disappointment. We only sulk with those we are emotionally close to. We are likely to sulk when someone close to us does not do what we want them to do, or does something we do not like, such as criticising, rejecting or disapproving, or depriving us of something. The function of sulking is to punish the other person; to get what we want; to extract proof of caring; to restore power; or to protect oneself from hurt.

This pattern of unhealthy communication has its roots in childhood experiences, where parents were likely to have avoided openly expressing negative feelings, and did not give the child permission to openly express direct anger. The sulking child punishes the parent by freezing them out, inviting them to cajole him or her out of it, but simultaneously being determined not to be appeased.

Be patient with the person who sulks. Do not say 'stop sulking', when they are sulking as this only makes matters worse – they are likely to retreat even further into their shell. Ask the person, when they are not sulking, how you can help.

Unhelpful beliefs underlying sulking

❶ **Demandingness or over-use of the words 'should', 'must' and 'ought'.** This 'should' not happen. The other person 'should' behave differently. I 'must' be treated well. People 'should' not get angry, or criticise me.

❷ **Catastrophising/awfulising.** 'The world is a terrible, awful place for allowing such a thing to happen', 'Isn't it awful', 'I can't bear it'.

❸ **All or nothing thinking.** 'That person is bad . . . they have rejected me . . . they do not accept me. I cannot accept the other person for being like they are . . . I cannot tolerate this feeling'.

Helpful beliefs

There are healthier, more constructive, alternatives to 'sulking' and these are the feelings of disappointment or anger. The person who feels disappointed thinks, 'I am a person in an unfortunate situation', which is subtly different

from the sulker who thinks, 'Poor me for receiving such treatment'. The person who expresses their annoyance in anger thinks, 'This is frustrating and I am going to tell somebody and do something about it'. Anger can at times be inappropriate, but if expressed carefully can help to identify and resolve problems. A healthier philosophy is based on the following key beliefs:

❶ It is undesirable to be treated unfairly, but it is not awful.

❷ I can stand this hurt and frustration and I can try to do something about the situation.

❸ I accept how the other person is. They may not have been rejecting me as a whole person but rather just one aspect of my behaviour.

❹ It is best to openly express my feelings; the consequences will not be as bad as I think.

Tactics for overcoming sulking

❶ Look at the advantages and disadvantages of sulking. Advantages might include, 'It lets him know that I'm angry', 'I feel more in control'. Disadvantages might be, 'It hides and avoids dealing with the real problem', 'It has a negative effect on our relationship'.

❷ Understand why you sulk. Think back to your childhood. Were you allowed to express your feelings openly, were you encouraged to be assertive?

❸ Analyse one specific episode of sulking at a time. Identify the most prominent feeling, eg, anger, disappointment, hurt. Pinpoint the aspect of the situation that you were most hurt by. Try to put into words and formulate in your own mind your interpretation of what happened, how you felt, and what you would like to be different.

❹ Express those negative feelings. Use the three-part assertive message. (1) 'I don't like it when you . . .' (2) 'It makes me feel . . .' (3) 'I would like it if . . .'

❺ Challenge unconstructive thinking patterns, particularly the overuse of the words 'should', 'ought' and 'must' and for your tendency to 'awfulise', and use 'all or nothing thinking'.

Communication is the life-blood of any relationship, without effective communication a relationship will wither and die. In the same way, a young baby's growth and development can be drastically arrested if denied human interaction and quality communication. Good communication consists of three essential skills.

◆ Listening to what the other person is saying.

◆ Expressing how you feel and what you think.

◆ Accepting the other person's opinions and feelings even when they are different from your own.

❶ Listening

Effective listening is an active, not passive, skill made up of a number of set components. The quality of our listening greatly affects the nature of the speaker's communication.

Five key listening skills

◆ Look at the person speaking.

◆ Be encouraging. Say, 'yes', 'hmmn', nod your head.

◆ Do not interrupt – be patient.

◆ Use open-ended questions. Say, 'how do you feel?' and not 'do you feel sad?'

◆ Reflect back and paraphrase the speakers emotions and meanings, eg, 'You must feel angry'.

❷ Communication spoilers

Behavioural scientists have identified particular types of communication spoilers which can have a negative effect on conversation.

Five key communication spoilers

◆ Judging, blaming, criticising or moralising.

◆ Name calling or put downs

◆ Interrupting

◆ Excessive questioning, using closed questions

◆ Offering solutions and solving problems rather than listening.

❸ Healthy communication

◆ Relationships are most healthy when both parties can openly and assertively express themselves.

◆ You accept that your partner can never be the same as you in the way he or she feels or thinks about things. Accepting how your partner is and tolerating the differences, and the resulting frustration, is an essential key for relationships to flourish.

❹ How to get your message across

Timing	Choose the right time and place. Not when you are very busy or tired. Make a special time.
Be concise	Stick to the issues. Do not lengthily trawl through old stale issues or nag.
Use the 'unselfish I' word	Beginning with 'I' shows that you accept full responsibility. Say 'I feel . . . or I think . . .', and not, 'You make me feel'.
Three-part assertive message	Describe: the behaviour; your feelings; and the effects, eg, 'When you leave your clothes on the floor, I feel annoyed, because it makes extra work. I would like it if . . .'
Choose the right words	Be positive. Avoid the tendency to insult, threaten or denigrate. Be honest but tactful. If you have to criticise others, criticise their actions not their character.
Keep your partner involved.	Make your point and encourage your partner to react. Keep in touch, listen to him or her.
Make notes	Beforehand, jot down the points you want to make.

❺ Gender differences in communication?

We might get angry with our partner because he or she does not communicate in the same way. But it has been suggested that men and women are fundamentally different in the way they communicate. Discuss these differences, if indeed they exist, with your partner.

MEN	WOMEN
Men offer solutions to problems, wanting to achieve results.	Women want to share feelings and discuss difficulties.
Men's talk is concerned with exhibiting knowledge, passing on information, preserving status and independence.	In women's talk the emphasis is on displaying similarity, establishing connections, and creating intimacy.
Men tend to think, internally and express the finished product of their thoughts.	Women tend to think aloud, sharing their inner dialogue.

P

SECTION 3 – MANAGING DEPRESSION

MANAGING DEPRESSION

■ Books for Professionals

Beck AT, Rush AJ, Shaw BF & Emery G, *Cognitive Therapy of Depression,* Guildford, New York, 1985 (paperback edition 1987).

Dryden W, *Developing Self-Acceptance*, John Wiley & Sons, Chichester, 1998.

Dryden W, *Rational Emotive Behavioural Therapy*, Winslow Press, Bicester, 1999.

Fennell M, 'Depression', Hawton K, Salkovskis P, Kirk J & Clark D (eds), *Cognitive Behaviour Therapy for Psychiatric Problems*, ch 6, Oxford University Press, Oxford, 1989.

McMullin R, *The New Handbook of Cognitive Therapy Technique*, Norton, London, 2000.

Williams JM, *The Psychological Treatment of Depression. A Guide to the Theory and Practice of Cognitive-Behavioural Therapy*. Croom Helm, London, 1984.

■ Books for Clients

Burns D, *Feeling Good – The New Mood Therapy*, New American Library, New York, 1980.

Burns D, *The Feeling Good Handbook: Using the New Mood Therapy in Everyday Life*, Penguin/Harpers & Row, New York, 1990.

Ellis A & Harper RA, *A New Guide to Rational Living*, Prentice Hall, New Jersey, 1975.

Gilbert P, *Overcoming Depression*, Robinson, London, 1997.

Greenberger D & Padesky C, *Mind over Mood*, Guildford Press, New York, 1995.

Holmes R & Holmes J, *The Good Mood Guide*, JM Dent, London, 1993.

Rowe D, *Depression, The Way Out of Your Own Prison*, Routledge, London, 1983.

Skynner R & Cleese J, *Families and How to Survive Them*, Methuen, London, 1983.

Tanner S & Bail J, *Beating the Blues – a Self-Help Approach to Overcoming Depression*, Sheldon Press, London, 1989.

■ Addresses

Compassionate Friends (for bereaved parents), 53 North Street, Bristol, Avon BS3 1EN. Tel 0117 953 9639 (helpline), 0117 966 5202 (advice)

CRUSE (Bereavement), Cruse House, 126 Sheen Road, Richmond, Surrey TW9 1UR Tel 020 8332 7227 and 020 8940 4818

'A problem that is well formulated is half resolved'
– Charles Wettering –

■ What is depression?

About 12 per cent of the population experience depression severe enough to require treatment at some time or other in their life.

People experience depression in many different ways, but perhaps the most prominent feature is a low or sad mood. Other typical signs of depression include lethargy, trouble with sleeping or early wakening, feeling constantly tired, pessimistic negative thoughts, difficulty thinking straight or making decisions, change in appetite and loss of interest. There are different types of depressive reaction ranging from mild mood fluctuations or 'the blues', to severe clinical depression. At the severe end of the scale people often experience more marked physical symptoms and it seems likely that this is related to biochemical changes in the brain.

For most people a depressive reaction is triggered by a set of life events which they are finding difficult to cope with. Depression is not easy to 'snap out of', but there are ways that you can gradually free yourself from depression.

■ Vulnerability to depression

Some people are more vulnerable to depression than others. A number of protective factors have been identified which can decrease vulnerability to depression.
These include:

◆ A high self-esteem based on self-worth, not achievements.

◆ Practising positive thinking habits.

◆ Assertively expressing your needs, thoughts and feelings.

◆ Using an established social support network.

◆ Stress management – balancing demands and resources and looking after yourself.

■ The depressive spiral – thoughts, mood, behaviour

Recent research has established that depressed people are prone to continuous, automatic, negative thoughts. Their thinking becomes distorted and they practise recognised thinking errors such as: 'all or nothing thinking', 'awfulising', 'personalising', 'focusing on the negative', and 'jumping to conclusions'. These patterns of thinking produce a low mood state which results in reduced activity. Reduced activity produces less rewarding experiences, which produces further negative thoughts and low mood. A vicious spiral of thoughts, feelings and behaviour is created. To arrest this downward spiral a number of things are necessary:

◆ *Understand the problem.* Understand the many factors both in the present and the past that have led you to feel the way you do.

◆ *Challenge negative thinking.* Recognise that the way that you think determines the way that you feel. Identify distorted thinking patterns and replace with more rational thoughts.

◆ *Increase activity levels.* Gradually increase your activity levels – particularly physical activity. Identify and work towards short and longer term goals.

◆ *Use support systems.* A close confiding relationship is the single most effective protection against depression. Talk about how you feel.

◆ *Assert yourself.* Express yourself assertively. Say 'no' to excessive demands. Look after your own needs.

Information about Depression

'Men are not worried by things, but by their ideas about things. When we meet with difficulties, become anxious or troubled, let us not blame others, but rather ourselves, that is, our ideas about things'

– Epictetus –

THOUGHTS
We make interpretations about these events by having a series of thoughts which continually flow through our minds. This is called our 'self-talk' or 'inner dialogue'.

ENVIRONMENT
We take in, and are aware of, a series of positive, negative and neutral events which are occurring all the time.

MOOD
Our feelings are created by our thoughts. All experiences are processed through our brains, interpreted and given meaning before we experience an emotional response.

◆ *Beliefs and thoughts.* Events themselves do not cause us to feel upset or depressed, rather it is our beliefs about these events that determine our emotional reaction. A network of fundamental beliefs influence our view of the world and our thinking patterns. It is important to be mindful about what we are thinking and to examine our underlying beliefs. We are thinking all of the time.

◆ *Selective bias in depression.* When we feel low in mood our thinking takes on a selective bias and we become more likely to think about negative things from the past. Low mood reactivates old negative thinking patterns. We then view the present more negatively and also view the future through a selective bias – like looking through a pair of dark glasses.

◆ *Recognise negative thinking.* Imagine you were feeling low in mood and when walking down the street you saw an acquaintance who just walked past you without acknowledging you. If you are feeling low you are likely to interpret this negatively – 'I must have done something wrong – they don't like me'. Your mind ignores other options such as 'they might be very busy' or 'they might have a problem which is preoccupying them'. The challenge when you are depressed is to step back and become mindful or aware of this process. Decentre yourself from the continuous chatter of your mind and challenge the process of thinking negatively automatically.

P

'There is nothing either good or bad, but thinking makes it so'

– Shakespeare –

EVENT

Girlfriend breaks the news that she wants to end their relationship.

THOUGHTS

INTERPRETATION OF EVENT

I can't stand living without her.

I must be a worthless person.

I'll never find a partner whom I will make happy.

She knew me and rejected me. There must be something seriously wrong with me.

I am too old to find another girlfriend. I'll be lonely for the rest of my life.

Awfulising

All or nothing

Jumping to conclusions

Personalising

Focusing on negatives

CHALLENGING IRRATIONAL THOUGHTS

It's painful at the moment. I feel sad and hurt but I can stand it.

There is no evidence that I am a worthless person.

That is definitely predicting the future and awfulising – I've been happy before and I am still the same person.

There is no evidence that there is anything seriously wrong – we were just different. There were things I didn't like about her.

Rubbish. There are plenty of people of my age in the same boat. Being alone for a while might be good for me anyway.

FEELINGS

DEPRESSION

NEW FEELINGS

SADNESS

I feel sad because I miss her and all the good times we had together. But I will get over these feelings – they won't last forever. In some ways it is good for me.

We are all prone at times to unhelpful 'distorted thinking', but when we are either under excess stress or are depressed, these distortions become more exaggerated. Research has shown that there are particular types of distorted thinking.

All-or-nothing thinking

You think in absolutes, as either black or white, good or bad, with no middle ground. You tend to judge people or events using general labels, for example 'he's an idiot', 'I'm hopeless. I'll never learn to drive. I'm a complete failure.' You may condemn yourself completely as a person on the basis of a single event.

Awfulising – catastrophising

You tend to magnify and exaggerate the important of events and how awful or unpleasant they will be, over-estimating the chances of disaster; whatever can go wrong will go wrong. If you have a setback you will view it as a never-ending pattern of defeat.

Personalising

You take responsibility and blame for anything unpleasant even if it has little or nothing to do with you. If something bad happens you immediately think 'it's my fault'.

Negative focus

You focus on the negative, ignoring or misinterpreting positive aspects of a situation. You focus on your weaknesses and forget your strengths, looking on the dark side. If you've done a good job, you filter out and reject the positive comments and focus on the negative.

Jumping to conclusions

You make negative interpretations even though there are no definite facts. You start predicting the future, and take on the mantle of 'mind reader'. You are likely to predict that negative things will happen.

Living by fixed rules

You tend to have fixed rules and unrealistic expectations, regularly using the words 'should', 'ought', 'must' and 'can't'. This leads to unnecessary guilt and disappointment. The more rigid these statements are, the more disappointed, angry, depressed or guilty you are likely to feel.

P

Please make an entry whenever you notice a definite drop in mood.

Diary Sheet

DATE/ TIME	DESCRIPTION OF SITUATION	MOOD LEVEL: 0–10	WHAT I WAS THINKING	ERRORS	CHALLENGES

Identify and name the common thinking distortions in each of the following statements. Underline the key words which point to a thinking distortion.

Jim is kept waiting 10 minutes for his appointment. As he sits waiting, he feels increasingly angry and tense. He thinks, 'These people should be on time. They just don't care about people like me. The trouble is they think they're better than me. I'll be stuck here all day.'

_____

Carol burns the apple pie while cooking a large four-course meal for Roger, her husband, and his business colleagues. She thinks, 'Oh no, the whole meal is ruined. I'm a hopeless cook and a complete failure as a wife. I should be a better wife to Roger.'

_____

Jane sees her friend Barbara walking along the other side of the road. Jane thinks, 'Barbara doesn't like me any more, she's ignoring me. I must have done something to upset her. I've never really had many friends – I guess I'm just not very likeable.'

_____

Tony is about to give a lecture and notices that he feels nervous. He thinks, 'Oh no – my mind will go blank – I'll dry up and won't be able to say anything. I'll make a complete fool of myself. This is going to be terrible.'

_____

Mary loses her temper and shouts at her six-year-old son, who has been playing after being told to tidy his bedroom. Mary thinks, 'Jonathan is really terrible – he's completely out of control – he won't do a thing I tell him to. He will end up a complete waster. I shouldn't lose my temper like that. I am a hopeless mother.'

_____

P

Listed below are a number of symptoms people have when they are feeling depressed.
Rate how you feel at the moment by placing an (X) at the appropriate point on each line.

EXAMPLE:

I feel very hot **X**————————————— I feel very cold

I do not feel ————————————— I feel so sad
unhappy I can't stand it

I feel very ————————————— I do not feel unusually
anxious anxious

I get no pleasure from ————————————— I still enjoy some
activities activities

I do not feel ————————————— I feel very
guilty guilty

I have no ————————————— I have energy and
energy motivation

I have difficulty thinking ————————————— I think as clearly
and making decisions as usual

I have disturbed sleep
(difficulty sleeping, ————————————— I sleep normally
early waking)

My appetite is ————————————— My appetite has
normal changed

I have constant negative ————————————— I think I am reasonably
thoughts about myself OK

I am as active ————————————— I am much less active
as usual than usual

I feel unusually emotional ————————————— I feel emotionally
and tearful well-balanced

I feel the future is ————————————— I do not feel discouraged
hopeless about the future

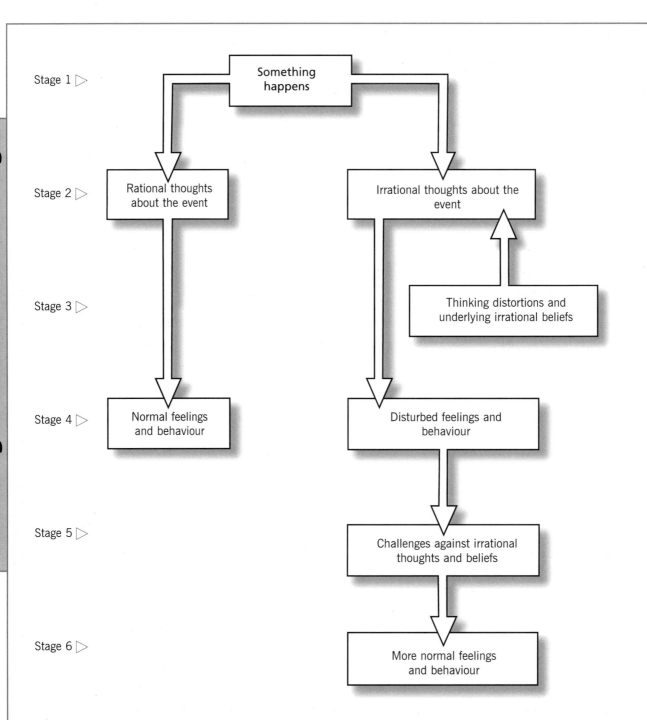

Stage 1 Note upsetting event.

Stage 2 List all rational and irrational thoughts about event.

Stage 3 Identify which thinking distortions you are making and which underlying irrational beliefs are behind your thoughts.

Stage 4 Note your disturbed feelings and behaviour.

Stage 5 Challenge and argue against your irrational thoughts.

Stage 6 Note differences in feelings and behaviour.

(Adapted from **Wycherley,** 1988)

P

EVENT/SITUATION CAUSING DISTRESS

I got angry and shouted at my six-year-old son when he continued to play with his toys after I had told him to tidy his room.

FEELING & ACTION TAKEN

Felt really angry and shouted at him, then felt really guilty and sulked around the house.

RATIONAL/IRRATIONAL THOUGHTS ABOUT THAT EVENT	THINKING DISTORTIONS	NEW RATIONAL CHALLENGES
He is really hopeless – completely out of control.	Awfulising All-or-nothing	He is a dreamer and is difficult to control but that's not so awful.
He did it on purpose – deliberately messing his room up more to upset me.	Personalising	No he didn't, he just got carried away with his play. It's only natural that six-year-olds find playing more interesting than tidying.
He takes absolutely no notice of me – he has no respect.	All-or-nothing	He does take notice most of the time. I know he loves me and I love him dearly.
He will end up as a complete waster, idling his life away.	Jumping to conclusions	I have no evidence of that – he might well be very creative.
Maybe I was too hard on him – I guess it's natural for kids that age to be untidy.	Rational	Yes, now that one sounds more rational.
I am a bad mother – I should be more patient.	All-or-nothing Awfulising Fixed Rules	Why am I a bad mother? I do lots of good things for him. I don't have to be perfect. It's quite normal for children to mess rooms up and for mothers to shout.
I'm a horrible person for losing my temper and shouting like that.	All-or-nothing Awfulising	I will try to control my temper, which is a weakness, but doesn't make me a horrible person.

UNDERLYING IRRATIONAL BELIEFS

I must be successful and competent in everything I do if I am to consider myself worthwhile.

When people act badly or unfairly I blame them and view them as completely bad and want them severely punished.

NEW FEELINGS & ACTION

Stop feeling so sorry and guilty and get on with my life.

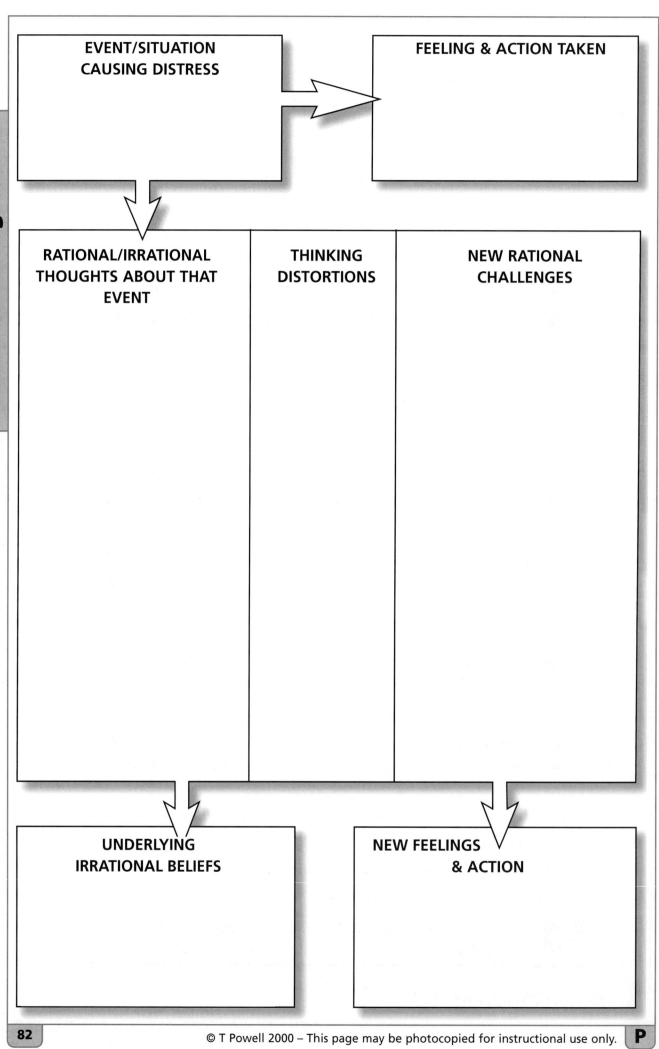

Event/Thinking Form

EVENT/SITUATION CAUSING DISTRESS	FEELING & ACTION TAKEN

RATIONAL/IRRATIONAL THOUGHTS ABOUT THAT EVENT	THINKING DISTORTIONS	NEW RATIONAL CHALLENGES

UNDERLYING IRRATIONAL BELIEFS	NEW FEELINGS & ACTION

P

Albert Ellis and his colleagues identified ten common irrational beliefs which, if held too rigidly, are likely to lead to emotional distress. These beliefs are learned early in life and become the bedrock from which our thinking patterns spring. Rate how strongly you hold any of these beliefs.

1 *I must be liked or accepted by every important person in my life, for almost everything I do.*

2 *I must be successful, competent and achieving in everything I do if I'm to consider myself worthwhile.*

3 *It is awful and terrible when things are not the way I would like them to be. Things should be different.*

4 *I must feel anxious, upset and preoccupied if something is, or may be, dangerous.*

5 *Human unhappiness is caused by events beyond our control so people have little or no ability to control their negative feelings.*

6 *It is easier to avoid facing many of life's difficulties and responsibilities than to face them.*

7 *The past is all-important, so if something once strongly affected one's life, it cannot be altered.*

8 *When people act badly, inadequately or unfairly, I blame them, and view them as completely bad or pathetic – including myself.*

9 *Maximum happiness can be achieved by inertia and inaction, or by passively enjoying oneself.*

10 *Everyone should be dependent on others and I need someone stronger than myself on whom I can rely.*

(Adapted from **Ellis & Harper,** 1975)

1 **I must be liked to accepted by every important person in my life, for almost everything I do.**

The approval of others is pleasant but not essential. In order to live life fully we need to express ourselves, which means that at times we will do things of which others disapprove. If we are constantly trying to avoid disapproval we will either become passive individuals or people with a poor sense of self. If, despite our efforts, we are disapproved of, the result can be devastating, because our self-esteem is based on what others think of us.

2 **I must be successful, competent and achieving in everything I do if I am to consider myself worthwhile.**

This means perpetually striving to do better and never being satisfied. Our value is directly equated to our achievements. The consequences are that we cannot relax, we feel useless if not working, and become perfectionists or immobilised by procrastination. We never achieve quite enough to feel really good because there is always something else. Again the net result is dissatisfaction. It is important to overcome the fear of failure and to view failure as something actually helpful.

3 **It is awful and terrible when things are not the way I would like them to be. Things should be different.**

This is the belief that life should be fair and just and satisfy our needs. Life is not fair and just. Holding this belief will mean that reality will be very painful and we will be constantly disappointed, angry, frustrated and depressed. Watch out for 'shoulds' and 'oughts' and learn to live with how things are, rather than how ideally we would like them to be, accepting our own limitations and the limitations of others. There is a wise saying that captures the essence of this belief: 'Let me have the determination to change what I can change, the serenity to accept what I cannot, and the wisdom to know the difference between the two'.

4 **I must feel anxious, upset and preoccupied if something is, or may be, dangerous.**

It is reasonable to take necessary steps to avoid danger. But excessive worry about things out of our control is unproductive. Watch out for 'awfulising', 'catastrophising' and 'wouldn't it be terrible if' thoughts. Often, even when the worst possible outcome is explored, it is still not as bad as we imagine. Being human is about overcoming groundless fears and anxieties.

5 **Human unhappiness is caused by events beyond our control so people have little ability to control their negative feelings.**

This belief can lead to passive acceptance of what fate brings when very often we can play a large part in controlling our own destiny. It also implies that 'someone out there' should sort things out. We can all influence our moods and how we feel; watch out for the thought, 'I can't help it, I'm just depressed'.

6 **It is easier to avoid facing many of life's difficulties and responsibilities than to face them.**

We can all waste our time hoping that something will magically work out rather than committing ourselves to positive action. Procrastination is largely about trying to avoid failure, but little is ever achieved without failure or risk. If we fail, have a bad experience or get hurt, we learn something. If we avoid these challenges, going for the easy option, we learn less and our confidence is gradually eroded.

7 **The past is all-important, so if something once strongly affected one's life, it cannot be altered.**

Thoughts like, 'That's just the way I am – I can't change' indicate this belief. Everybody can learn new skills all the time. It does not necessarily mean that we will be very good at those skills, but mostly we can achieve competence. We can all change the way we behave to some extent. Imagine your life as a film with you as the director and script writer; rewrite your own script.

8 **When people act badly, inadequately or unfairly, I blame them and view them as completely bad or pathetic – including myself.**

This touches on our tendency to expect others to behave in the way that we want them to, or think that they should behave. But ask yourself, 'Why should they behave in that way?' The more rigidly we hold these expectations for others the more disappointed and angry we will become when they let us down. If we have these expectations for ourselves it can lead us to feeling excessively guilty and depressed. We also have a tendency to blame and condemn people totally on the basis of our observation on aspects of their behaviour. We might say, 'He's absolutely hopeless', if for example, a colleague turns up late for a meeting. What would be more logical would be to describe his specific behaviour and say, 'He's a poor timekeeper', rather than making such a dismissive generalisation.

9 **Maximum happiness can be achieved by inertia and inaction, or by passively enjoying oneself.**

People who say that they are bored often hold this belief. There is an expectation that there are lots of interesting things out there to entertain and keep us all happy. If we just sit back and expect to be entertained we will not feel satisfied. Real satisfaction, in the long term, comes from active participation and skill development rather than passively receiving. Getting actively involved and committed means taking risks, facing new experiences and facing fears. What you get out is proportional to what you put in.

10 **Everyone should be dependent upon others and I need someone stronger than myself on whom I can rely.**

This belief often produces the thought, 'I cannot live without somebody', but the reality is that we all can. This belief distracts us from learning to live with ourselves first and diminishes our own personal sense of power.

(Adapted from **Ellis & Harper,** 1975)

 P

Write down on a piece of paper all your negative thoughts and then challenge them.

NEGATIVE THOUGHT	CHALLENGE
I can't stand it.	I can stand it. It's difficult but I can put up with it. It is good for me.
I am just not good enough.	I am not perfect. Like everybody I am good at some things and not so good at others.
What is the point trying?	If I don't try, I won't know. Trying in itself will broaden my experience and skill. Nobody is expecting me to do it perfectly.
What if I make a mistake – it would be awful.	Everybody makes mistakes. It is good to make mistakes because that is the best way to learn.
I have nothing to say – I'm boring.	I have opinions, thoughts and feelings. I like reading and going out. Perhaps I need to improve my ability to express myself. I can practice.
If people really knew me they wouldn't like me.	There are things about me that are likeable and things that are unlikeable – just like everybody else.
Nobody likes me.	There are people who like me. I have had better relationships in the past and will in the future.
Everybody else has a better time than I do – they're all happy.	I don't know this for a fact. Just because they seem busier doesn't mean they are more satisfied.
It would be best if I stayed away from people because I'm no good at relationships.	If I stay away I don't give myself a chance. I'll probably be all right if I can just relax.
I might break down emotionally in front of people and feel ridiculous.	I have a good reason to be upset. People are a lot more understanding than I think. It would not be the end of the world. What is wrong with showing emotion?
I'm hopeless at everything. I'll never sort myself out like this.	Just take one stop at a time. Totally condemning myself is nonsense. I've overcome more difficult problems than this.

■ Situation

Feeling rather down and anxious, 24 hours before running my first national three-day workshop. I can't quite put my finger on what is wrong. Now, what am I thinking? I write down my key thoughts and realise they are somewhat distorted. After challenging these thoughts I feel more positive.

THOUGHTS	CHALLENGES
I haven't prepared properly – I've still got so much to do – I'll never do it all.	Richard said don't over-prepare. I will spend the next couple of hours preparing the first session and then tomorrow I'll spend one hour on an overview and I should be all right.
I don't feel very well – I think I'm coming down with flu. Oh no, they will never find a replacement at such short notice. It would be awful running a three-day workshop whilst feeling terrible.	I always feel under the weather before a stressful event. Remember all those marathons I used to run. Almost every time, the night before I thought I'd pulled a muscle or got flu, but I was always all right on the day. Anyway, even if I am ill I could still do it. Remember giving that lecture when I was actually sick – I managed.
All this material is a load of rubbish. I really don't have any great faith in it.	The material is OK. I've been using it for the last six years – clients find it helpful. It's not the universal panacea for everything, but it's useful.
What if they are an unfriendly, critical group of people? It would be terrible if I was heckled or made fun of for three days.	It is unlikely that a bunch of OTs, community nurses and social workers will be hypercritical. Think of the OTs and CPNs I know – they are all nice people.
They will find this material and me really boring. I wish I was a funnier person.	The material is not boring. I would have been very interested in it all six years ago. Louise and Simon thought it was good. If Richard can run one of these workshops without boring people stiff, so can I. Anyway these people are coming to learn, not to be entertained.
What if I get so nervous that my mind goes completely blank?	I've given scores of talks and lectures before – my mind has never gone blank. If I forget what I'm going to say, I can always put an overhead on.

P

> '**Action may not always bring happiness; but there is no happiness without action**'
>
> *– Benjamin Disraeli –*

■ The problem

Feeling depressed is a vicious spiral. Your negative thoughts make you feel miserable, inadequate and discouraged, which means you feel slowed down and tired and less inclined to be active. Your activity level goes down; you start to avoid situations, which means that you don't have positive thoughts and experiences; your confidence is further reduced, which increases the negative thoughts and low mood and so on the less you do, the less you want to do.

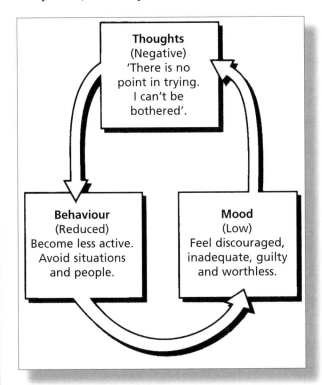

■ The way out

Becoming more active is one way of breaking this vicious depressive spiral because:

Activity makes us feel less tired

Normally when you feel tired you need a rest but when you are feeling depressed the opposite is true – you need to do more. Doing nothing makes you feel more exhausted and lethargic.

Activity distract us

Being active gives your mind something different to think about instead of dwelling on worrying negative thoughts when you are inactive.

Activity improves our confidence

Being active gives you more of a sense that you are taking control of your life again and achieving something worthwhile. Small steps help rebuild shattered confidence. Then there is a chain reaction effect where you feel motivated to try to achieve something else.

Activity improves our thinking

Activity improves our thinking and memory and helps us to get problems into a more realistic perspective.

Activity can involve others

People who care about you will probably be pleased to see you more active, which may make you feel better. Being more involved with people improves your chances of feeling better.

■ What to do

Begin by setting yourself simple tasks, such as making a phone call or doing the shopping. Jot down a list of tasks that are 'out of grasp but not out of reach'. Accept that the tasks are difficult and require effort. Being depressed is a little like having flu – you feel sluggish, its an effort. Do not expect to find these activities immediately enjoyable – nevertheless it is a first step.

Using an activity diary

Keeping a diary of daily activities can be especially useful when you are depressed because it helps you to focus on how you are spending your time, reminds you what you have done, and is a useful way of planning ahead. Use the weekly diary sheet on the next page.

❶ **Plan what you are going to do the next day:** Write down a list of activities that you would like to do and then schedule them into the diary. It is helpful to do this the night before and to plan each part of the day on an hourly basis.

❷ **Plan activities that are absorbing and not too difficult:** If you are feeling depressed it is sometimes difficult to become absorbed by reading a book but is more easily to be absorbed by for example watching a video (see Pleasant Activity List).

❸ **Plan a mixture of activities that have a balance between duty and pleasure:** Try to introduce more pleasurable items into your schedule. These might include small items such as having a leisurely bath, or larger items such as going out and meeting a friend.

❹ **Break tasks down into smaller steps:** Do not tidy the whole house, but rather break it down into 'vacuum lounge carpet' or 'tidy kitchen surfaces'.

❺ **Plan activities that increase your physical activity levels:** For instance, walking the dog or walking to the shop, mowing the lawn or cycling. Physical activities are very important for producing brain chemicals that are natural anti-depressants. Research shows that exercise has a positive effect on people's mood and releases feelings of tension, frustration and anger. Exercise also improves sleeping, physical health and the body's immune system.

❻ **Be flexible:** Try to keep to your plan as much as possible but allow yourself flexibility. If you have missed an activity proceed to the next one.

❼ **Increase frequency:** the number of activities that you do during the day, building up very slowly.

❽ **Record your sense of pleasure (P) and achievement (A) for each activity:** Rate both pleasure and achievement on a scale of 0 to 5, where 5 is either much pleasure or much achievement and 0 is no pleasure or no achievement.

❾ **Work towards goals:** Work out a number of short and long-term goals for different areas of your life. This helps activity planning and increases motivation. Always write your goals down.

Achieving everyday tasks

Being depressed often means that you have put off doing the simplest of things. These small jobs pile up and sometimes you might feel overwhelmed. The following steps are to help you reduce this mountain and turn it into smaller molehills.

❶ Write down on a list all the tasks that you feel you need to do.

❷ Prioritise. Do not try to do everything at once, only do one thing at a time. Identify what needs to be done first.

❸ Break the task down into specific steps.

❹ Rehearse each task, picture yourself performing the task in your mind.

❺ Anticipate difficulties. Write down any practical difficulties that might come up.

❻ Deal with negative thoughts. Identify the negative thoughts and then challenge them.

❼ Start at the beginning.

❽ Reward yourself for your success. Tick off the things that you have achieved and reward yourself with small rewards throughout the day such as a coffee, watching your favourite television programme or reading the newspaper.

P

Weekly Activity Schedule

WEEK BEGINNING _____ NAME _____

	MONDAY	TUESDAY	WEDNESDAY	THURSDAY	FRIDAY	SATURDAY	SUNDAY
Wake–9am							
9am–10am							
10am–11am							
11am–12 noon							
12 noon–1pm							
1pm–2pm							
2pm–3pm							
3pm–4pm							
4pm–5pm							
5pm–6pm							
6pm–7pm							
7pm–8pm							
8pm–9pm							
9pm–bed							

✓ *Place a tick next to any activity you would be prepared to pursue in the next week.*

○ *Place a circle next to any activity you would like to try in the next few months.*

List of Pleasant Events

■ Social activities

- [ ] Visit somebody
- [ ] Write a letter or a card
- [ ] Telephone a friend
- [ ] Go out for a social drink
- [ ] Go to a restaurant
- [ ] Invite a friend around
- [ ] Buy a present for somebody
- [ ] Ask for a cuddle
- [ ] Be with children
- [ ] Do something for somebody
- [ ] Have a good conversation
- [ ] Be with my family
- [ ] Give a party
- [ ] Go to a party
- [ ] Make a new friend
- [ ] Compliment or praise somebody
- [ ] Be with someone you love

■ Recreational activities

- [ ] Go to church
- [ ] Go to the zoo, fair or circus
- [ ] Go for a walk
- [ ] Listen to music
- [ ] Read a novel, magazine or newspaper
- [ ] Go to the cinema
- [ ] Go for a jog
- [ ] Gardening
- [ ] Go swimming
- [ ] Play a sport
- [ ] Have a sauna
- [ ] Watch a sports event
- [ ] Play a game
- [ ] Visit a place of interest
- [ ] Visit the countryside
- [ ] Plan a holiday
- [ ] Sit in the sun
- [ ] Go fishing
- [ ] Play a board game
- [ ] Plan a day out
- [ ] Go to a health club
- [ ] Go on a nature walk
- [ ] Clean out a cupboard
- [ ] Be with animals

■ Creative activities

- [ ] Write a poem
- [ ] Paint a picture
- [ ] Cook a meal
- [ ] Decorate a room
- [ ] Play an instrument
- [ ] Do some DIY
- [ ] Sewing or knitting
- [ ] Make a model
- [ ] Write a diary
- [ ] Sing a song
- [ ] Pick flowers
- [ ] Sit in the sun
- [ ] Rearrange the furniture
- [ ] Paint a room
- [ ] Dance
- [ ] Restore an antique

■ Self-care activities

- [ ] Buy something for myself
- [ ] Wear something nice
- [ ] Relax in a warm bath
- [ ] Have a massage or sauna
- [ ] Watch a favourite television programme
- [ ] Go to the hairdresser
- [ ] Buy food I like
- [ ] Put on make up, do hair
- [ ] Take a nap
- [ ] Set a goal, make a plan
- [ ] Talk about something I like
- [ ] Sleep in late
- [ ] Buy a takeway meal

■ Educational activities

- [ ] Go to the library
- [ ] Go to the museum
- [ ] Enrol on a course
- [ ] Read a non-fiction book
- [ ] Do a crossword or puzzle
- [ ] Learn something new
- [ ] Learn a foreign language
- [ ] Learn to play a musical instrument
- [ ] Go to a lecture
- [ ] Buy a book

P

We are all prone to 'demanding thinking', using the words, 'should', 'ought' and 'must', to some extent. However, the more we are inclined to use these words, in our internal thinking or our speech, the more pressure or stress we apply to ourselves. At the moment I am thinking, 'I should finish this section of the book this week' and 'I should spend more time with the children'. The more 'shoulds' and 'oughts' we have weighing down on our shoulders, the more we are likely to feel frustration, disappointment, anger, guilt and depression. The word 'should' can be traced back to the Anglo-Saxon word 'sceolde'; undoubtedly we are scolding ourselves when we use the word. The worst should of all is probably; 'I should be successful at everything that I strive to do'. This puts an almost impossible burden upon us.

To a large extent we learn this type of thinking from our childhood. The more rigid these beliefs, the more critical we are likely to be towards ourselves or others. Try the following exercises to 'loosen up' or delete some of these shoulds from your internal vocabulary.

■ Exercise

❶ Make a list of five 'should' statements about how you think you ought to be:

1 *I should* _____

2 _____

3 _____

4 _____

5 _____

❷ Make a list of five statements about how you think others ought to be:

1 *Other people should* _____

2 _____

3 _____

4 _____

5 _____

❸ **Challenge:** Take the most demanding should statement from each section and challenge it. Where does this should come from? Who is it who says I should? Where is it written that I should ? Why should I? What is so important?

❹ **Carry out a cost benefit analysis:** Write down a list of what the advantages and disadvantages of having this rule are.

❺ **Bring on the substitute:** Rewrite the statements substituting a different phrase for 'should'. For example 'it would be nice if... ', or 'I would prefer it if...'.

❻ **'Should' busting:** Take five minutes out of every day to recite or write down all your should, must and ought statements. This will hopefully help you to see how unhelpful, if not ridiculous, most of these statements are.

Overcoming the Tyranny of the 'Shoulds'

**'He is a man who is impossible to please,
because he is never pleased with himself'**

– Goethe –

The perfectionist is a person who has to get everything just right – somebody who has excessively high standards. Most of us reach a stage in a task where putting in more effort will only bring very marginal gains. We recognise that this is the time to stop and focus on something more profitable. The perfectionist has difficulty letting things go, and varying standards according to time available and effort needed. Perfection is an unobtainable illusion guaranteed to make us feel like failures and make us vulnerable to depression.

Behind perfectionism lurk deep unrecognised fears and needs. The perfectionist is motivated by a fear of failure. In failing to reach a goal, he or she feels a failure as a person. The perfectionist is never satisfied by achievements, needing to constantly strive for more and more. The perfectionist is also somebody who keeps emotions under tight control and has a fear of showing vulnerability or loosing control. On the other hand, the person with a healthy pursuit of excellence is motivated by enthusiasm, generally feels OK about themselves, is not afraid of failing and can show vulnerability.

Consider three benefits of not being perfect or making a mistake:

a We learn from mistakes – we will not learn unless we make mistakes.

b Most people are more comfortable with 'imperfect', vulnerable people.

c If we fear making a mistake we often become paralysed into inaction, afraid to do anything.

■ Exercise

❶ **List advantages and disadvantages:** Show that perfectionism does not in fact help you by listing the advantages and disadvantages of perfectionism in you.

ADVANTAGES	DISADVANTAGES
Produce high quality work	*Never satisfied so often feel tense.*
_____	*Difficulty varying work speed.*
_____	*Critical of self and others.*
_____	*Avoids risks and new things.*
_____	_____
_____	_____

❷ **Deliberately limit time and lower standards:** Identify a task and set a time limit for it so that you cannot do the job perfectly. Instead of saying, ' I am going to write a letter or report', try saying, 'I'm going to write this in 15 minutes'. Instead of saying, 'I'm going to tidy the house', say, 'I have got half an hour to tidy the house, that means 5 minutes on each room'. Attempt a task at 80 per cent of your normal level.

❸ **Disclose weakness:** Make a deliberate attempt to disclose to others your weaknesses or vulnerabilities. If you are nervous or inadequate in a situation say so. Treat this as a challenge. Dare to be average and admit it. Notice how others react. Do they seem more comfortable?

❹ **Deliberately savour the moment:** Try to focus more on the process of doing something rather than the outcome. Stop and enjoy the moment rather than concentrating on the end result.

 P

'People are lonely because they build walls instead of bridges'

– Joseph Newton –

1 *Recognise your thinking distortions. When your mood is low there is a tendency for your thinking to become distorted (all-or-nothing, exaggerated, etc). Note the following common thoughts associated with loneliness and identify thinking distortions: 'I have no friends', 'No one likes or loves me', 'What good am I to anybody?', 'Nobody understands me', 'I need to be loved', 'I am boring.'*

2 *Stop comparing yourself with others. Again look out for thinking distortions, 'Everyone is busier and happier than me', 'Everybody else has fulfilling relationships'. You have an idealised fantasy about other people's lives which means that there is no way your own life will match up.*

3 *Recognise the vicious spiral of low mood, and how it has led to you withdrawing from other people because of your fear of hurt and rejection. Turn this process around and start approaching others rather than avoiding. Plan activities that increase your social contacts. Contact people you know and like. Talk to neighbours. Develop a hobby.*

4 *Recognise the difference between being alone and loneliness. Don't equate alone with loneliness. Learn to enjoy doing things and caring for yourself on your own. Cook yourself a nice meal, play your favourite music, read a good book. The more you can feel at home with yourself – not looking around for others all the time – the more attractive a person you will become. People who have found happiness in themselves are often the most desired.*

5 *Plan a variety of activities to do on your own (eg, go to an art gallery or walk in the park). Before you carry out the activity draw up a chart and rate how satisfying you think it will be on a scale of 0 to 100 (0 = no satisfaction, 100 = enormous satisfaction). Then, after you've carried out the activity, rate the actual satisfaction.*

6 *List some advantages of being alone, starting with, 'It provides an opportunity to explore how I really feel and think'; 'It allows me to develop personal strength'.*

Six Ways to Overcome Loneliness

'Beware of Jealousy. It is the green eyed monster which does mock the meat it feeds on'

– Othello –

■ What underlies jealousy?

The first and primary fear in jealousy is that of losing something important, whether it be an important relationship, control or status. Underlying this fear is usually a deep-seated feeling of insecurity and a lack of confidence. Jealous people often lack confidence in themselves and have difficulty believing that somebody else can love them for themselves. Very often the person who suffers from jealousy has had a childhood where they felt that they were never really unconditionally loved for who they were, instead they often base their feelings of self worth on what they do. To make themselves feel better they base their feelings of worth on either external achievements, physical attractiveness or possessions. Rejection or losing possessions, or a relationship breaking down, is devastating because it leaves the jealous person feeling worthless.

The second fear associated with jealousy is the fear of change, often triggered by a change in the relationship as the other partner develops or grows in some way. The sub-conscious irrational thought here is that change is always for the worst. Very often this person's childhood has been characterised by an avoidance of change, adventure or spontaneity – change spells danger.

A further fear is that of being alone and this is often related to past feelings of abandonment and lack of trust in the partner's ability to stay in the relationship. Often somewhere in the person's past he or she has felt painfully excluded or abandoned.

■ Characteristics of jealous relationships

The jealous person has an inbuilt attentional bias and is constantly scanning their environment for signs of infidelity. As with any hypervigilance 'the more you look, the more you will find'. This needs to be modified. The jealous person might also deliberately avoid jealousy-provoking situations, such as social events; again this needs to be reversed.

Relationships where there is a great deal of possessive jealousy often have a number of unhealthy characteristics. There is sometimes a master/slave mentality where a partner is seen as a possession or something to own, or control, rather than a free, growing individual. Secondly, there is often the rather naive notion that people love each other unconditionally and continue to do so irrespective of one person's behaviour. The lesson needs to be learnt that you will drive them away – you are damaging your relationship. Thirdly, there is often a lack of care about the other's feelings and a blind spot as to how the jealous, persecutory behaviour makes the other person feel.

P

1 *Accept that you have a problem and take responsibility for it*. It is no use continuously blaming your partner. Nobody can make you jealous, you do it to yourself. Say, 'I feel insecure ... worried ...' rather than accusing and interogating.

2 *Set limits on your own behaviour with your partner*. Try to keep your thoughts and accusations to yourself, and if you are going to get jealous agree to show it for a limited period of say twenty minutes and then stop. Make an agreement with your partner that they will not tolerate an inquisition – encourage them to get tough.

3 *Challenge your irrational thinking patterns* for cognitive distortions such as 'all or nothing' thinking, 'awfulising', 'personalising', and 'jumping to conclusions'. So challenge the thought: 'He really likes Linda, he is going to have an affair with her'. Find the middle ground, the grey area.

4 *Build up your own self-esteem.* Write down a list of positive statements about yourself from the other person's perspective. For example, my partner likes me because: I have got a nice smile, he finds me sexually attractive, etc.

5 *Explore life without jealousy.* How would your relationship be different if this problem of jealousy magically disappeared. Sometimes jealousy can serve as a focus. Explore other potential problems.

6 *Develop your own independence.* The less you rely on your partner the better you will feel about yourself. Do things that you enjoy and create a healthy distance between you and your partner – this will make you feel closer. Learn to trust rather than control.

7 *Make links between these feelings and your childhood.* Try to understand the voices from the past and the roots of these powerful feelings.

'Give sorrow words: for the grief that does not speak knits up the o'er wrought heart, and bids it break'

– Macbeth –

The word bereavement means, 'to be robbed of something valued'. Grieving is a process of adjusting to that loss and is universal. Although most often applied when the loss involves a death it can be applied to many other situations.

■ Bereavement is a process

People pass through a number of **stages in grief,** which can vary in sequence and length for each individual.

◆ **Stage One – Shock.** The reality of the loss takes time to sink in. Initial reactions vary from numbness, denial, disbelief, hysteria, to not being able to think straight. These natural reactions cushion us against the loss and allow us to feel it more slowly and cope with it better.

◆ **Stage Two – Protest.** At this stage the person protests that the loss cannot be real. Strong and powerful feelings occur, such as anger, guilt, sadness, fear, yearning and searching, while the person struggles between denying and accepting the reality of what has happened.

◆ **Stage Three – Disorganisation.** This is the stage when the reality of the loss is only too real. This is the low point of the wheel of grief, characterised by bleakness, despair, depression, apathy, anxiety and confusion. The person may feel that the feelings will go on forever.

◆ **Stage Four – Reorganisation.** The person begins to rebuild a life, acquiring more balance and being able to choose to remember happier times. The person returns to previous functioning, but often with changed values and new meaning in life.

■ Tasks involved in grieving

❶ **Accepting the loss:** The starting point of grief is intellectually and emotionally to accept the loss. At first the loss is not taken in and, for example, the grieving individual may keep all the person's belongings. It takes time for those possessions to be let go.

❷ **Feeling the pain:** This means allowing an array of emotions to be allowed, recognised and experienced. The pain of grief is very real, and as with any pain we try to avoid it, but it is an essential part of the process and must be acknowledged and worked through. Some people will try to avoid that pain by keeping themselves very busy. Other people might defend themselves against the pain by saying to themselves, 'I've got to be strong for everybody else'. Crying about it is undoubtedly helpful as it allows painful feelings to be expressed.

❸ **Talking about it:** Talking it over and over, and reminiscing helps it to sink in. Talking about regrets, expressing fears and anger is helpful. Do not take the attitude that 'it doesn't help to rake it up'. The listener often just needs to be present to listen, and encourage talk of the deceased.

❹ **Take one day at a time:** It helps to focus on now, and not to try to take on everything at once. Grieving takes the time it takes, there are no fixed time limits and it is not a process that can be hurried. Do not feel, 'I should have got over this by now'. Expect anniversaries to be times when sad feelings are rekindled.

❺ **Be your own best friend:** Look after yourself; rest, eat well, take time to retreat and time to talk, try not to become too isolated but seek out social support.

❻ **Exercise: a letter from the heart:** When someone dies everyone has things they wished they had said. Write a letter expressing all your feelings; write about the good things and the bad things, the things you most liked and the things you least liked, the things you could never talk about, write about how you will remember the deceased. Say goodbye.

P

The skill of 'looking after ourselves', and paying attention to our needs is an important one. It involves being assertive enough to say, 'This is what I like', 'This is what I need', being able to say 'no' to the requests of others, and being able to 'treat' ourselves, by giving ourselves pleasure. Some people have never learned to look after themselves in this way; they might feel guilty and view it as being selfish.

The word 'selfish' has a negative connotation for most people. Certainly putting yourself first, always ignoring the needs of others is undesirable. However, a philosophy of enlightened self-interest, or being interested in ourselves as well as others, is desirable. Sometimes it may be necessary to be selfish to ensure there is a balance between our own needs and those of others.

HOW GOOD ARE YOU AT LOOKING AFTER YOURSELF?

Scoring:

3 Very like me	2 Like me	1 Unlike me	0 Very unlike me

1	I occasionally give myself something nice like a present or treat	
2	I make time to do relaxing activities	
3	I believe it is necessary to be selfish at times	
4	I like it when others look after me when I am ill	
5	I plan events in my life that I can look forward to, such as holidays and outings	
6	Every day I make sure I have some time to do something pleasurable for myself	
7	I make a point of looking after my appearance and health	
8	I like it when somebody gives me a present or compliments me on something I've done	
9	I can praise myself if I think that I have done a good job	
10	I feel in control of my life, I do not simply live my life according to what other people want	
11	I make a point of eating a healthy diet and do not skip meals	
12	I deliberately engage in exercise and keep myself physically fit	
13	I deliberately make time to cultivate friendships with people I like	
14	I make time to engage in absorbing, meaningful hobbies and activities	
15	Sometimes I have to put my own needs first which means I may have to hurt others	
16	I can say 'no' when other people make demands on me	

Scoring: Score less than 25 = you certainly need to improve your self care skills.
Homework task: Draw up a list of 10 treats, pleasant activities, or things that you like and gradually introduce them into your weekly timetable.

1 *This is it! There are no rehearsals or preparations. Your life is on and running.*

2 *There is no way that you can get everything that you want. You may satisfy some of your needs, but you will always feel some dissatisfaction.*

3 *You cannot completely control or own anything, particularly people. Everything is temporary and everything changes. Get used to change.*

4 *Nobody is stronger or weaker than anybody else. We are all made up of a collection of strengths and weaknesses.*

5 *All important decisions are made on the basis of limited information. Everything has an element of risk.*

6 *All life's important battles and conflicts are fought within ourselves.*

7 *You are responsible for everything that you do. All excuses are unacceptable.*

8 *We all make mistakes; we are all selfish, cheating, vain, greedy and tell lies. We are all human. Nobody is perfect. Learn to forgive yourself and accept your humanness.*

9 *We are all free to do whatever we like; all we have to do is face the consequences.*

10 *The world is not always just or fair. Being good offers no guarantee of a happy outcome.*

P

1 ***Take responsibility.*** *You are responsible for your own life and everything in it, including your own happiness. Do not blame your parents, your childhood, society, others or life events.*

2 ***Be flexible in your thinking****. Beware of absolutist, 'all or nothing', 'black and white', rigid thinking, with an over-emphasis on the words 'should', 'must', 'ought' and 'can't'. Loosen up your thinking, look at alternative views, avoid perfectionism.*

3 ***Confront rather than avoid difficulties and frustration****. Treat problems as challenges, as useful in helping you to build up a tolerance and experience. Expect change and challenges and for life to be unfair at times.*

4 ***Look after your own needs.*** *Be assertive in identifying and meeting your own needs, whether it be for food, exercise, relaxation, pleasure, work, laughter or love. We all need to have good self-care skills.*

5 ***Express yourself****. Express positive feelings of love, joy and excitement, but also negative feelings of anger, sadness and disappointment. Always be willing to 'talk about things', try not to 'bottle things up' or avoid issues.*

6 ***Strive for balance.*** *Feel in control of your life by making active choices and decisions about how you spend your time. Fill your life with a balance of work and play, time alone and with people, and physical and mental activity.*

7 ***Develop and maintain relationships.*** *Value and nurture friendships. Develop a network of social support and confiding relationships as they act as an insulator against stress. Accept others for how they are, rather than trying to change them.*

We all need goals to work towards.
A lack of goals inevitably leads to feelings of depression.
Goals provide a sense of meaning and motivation – without them our lives
tend to lose meaning and we tend to lose motivation. Achieving goals helps
to give your confidence a boost. Make sure the goals you set are not
overwhelming, are interesting and challenging.

GOAL AREA	SHORT TERM *(Next few weeks)*	MID TO LONG TERM *(Next few months)*
WORK		
LEISURE/PERSONAL DEVELOPMENT/ HEALTH		
FAMILY & DOMESTIC		

P

SECTION 4 – MANAGING STRESS

MANAGING STRESS

■ Books for Professionals and Clients

Adair J, *Effective Time Management,* Pan, London, 1982.

Adams JD, *Understanding and Managing Stress: A Book of Readings*, University Associates Inc, San Diego, California, 1980.

Bailey R, *50 Activities for Managing Stress*, Gower, Aldershot, 1991.

Butler G & Hope T, *Manage your Mind*, Oxford University Press, Oxford, 1995.

Charlesworth EA & Nathan RG, *Stress Management*, Souvenir Press, London, 1982.

Cohen-Posey K, *Brief Therapy Client Handouts*, John Wiley & Sons, New York, 2000.

Cooper C, Cooper R & Eaker L, *Living with Stress*, Penguin, London, 1988.

Covey S, *The Seven Habits of Highly Effective People*, Simon & Schuster, New York, 1989.

Cox T, *Stress*, Macmillan Press, London, 1978.

Davis M, Eshelman E & McKay M, *The Relaxation and Stress Workbook*, New Harbinger, Oakland, Ca, 1995.

Drucker P, *The Effective Executive*, Heinemann, London, 1967.

Holmes TH & Rahe RH, 'The Social Adjustment Rating Scale', *Journal of Psychosomatic Research* 11, pp213–18, 1967.

Powell T, *Stress Free Living*, Dorling Kindersley, London, 2000.

Selye H, *Stress Without Distress*, Lipincott, Philadelphia, 1974.

Totman R, *Mind, Stress and Health*, Souvenir Press, London, 1990.

References

Life as an ocean liner

Imagine that your life is like an ocean going liner and you are the captain. For that liner to be sea-worthy and stay afloat in stormy weather, various parts of the ship are separated into compartments. If the ship is damaged and one areas starts taking on water that damage is restricted to that one compartment. This is quite a good way of looking at your own life. Most of us have different areas in our lives such as family, friends, hobbies or work. Some people have more overlap than others; some people live very compartmentalised lives. One definite advantage of a compartmentalised life is that if one area or compartment of your life goes wrong, it doesn't mean your whole life has to. So if something goes wrong at work and you have an all-consuming hobby, such as sailing, music, playing golf or painting, for example, you can get away from the areas of stress and be absorbed by another area.

It is a great thing to be able to think about something completely different when worried by a particular stress. If you have difficulties in your relationship with your partner, but can turn to your family or a friend this again reduces the stress. It does however take a deliberate consistent effort, time and energy to develop and maintain these separate compartments.

Exercise

Review each area of your life in the diagram below. Write in the names of people, whether they are friends or family and specific activities or hobbies. Ask yourself how much time and energy you put into each area. Do you have separate areas in your life? Add any special area that you have in the empty box or draw your own ocean liner, with the different size compartments to reflect your own life.

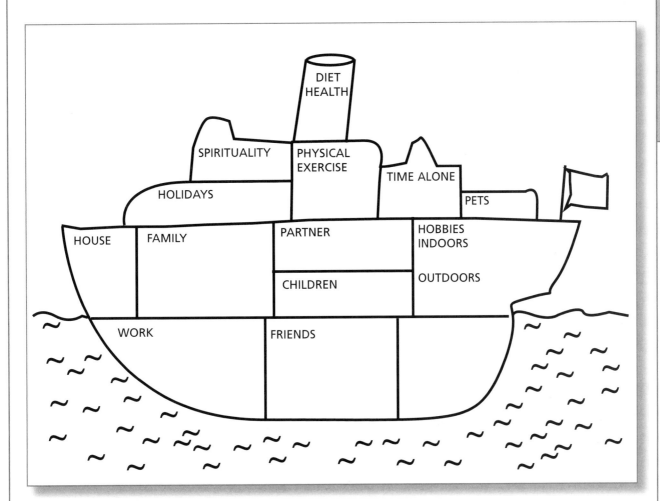

Understand more about stress

Recognise your major sources of stress at present.

Understand how stress affects you.

Anticipate and plan for periods of stress.

Find your optimal level – not too much or too little.

Adopt a systematic problem – solving approach

Define your problem specifically – try to be objective.

Break it down into manageable components.

Approach projects one stage at a time.

Develop, evaluate and execute a course of action.

Recognise and accept your own feelings

Express the way you are feeling openly with others.

Accept your feelings.

Be aware of past experiences which effect your feelings.

Develop new effective behavioural skills

Be assertive – learn to say 'No'.

Avoid procrastination. 'Do it today!'

Manage your time effectively.

Avoid being a perfectionist.

Practice rational thinking

Delegate effectively.

Practice goal planning.

Establish and make use of a good social support network

Ask for help and accept it when offered.

Deliberately cultivate good relationships.

Talk to people: family, old friends, new friends.

Maintain a healthy lifestyle

Take regular physical exercise.

Maintain a healthy balanced diet.

Deliberately seek out change of pace, and new activities in your life.

Make time to relax and enjoy yourself

Set aside time each day to do something you enjoy.

Plan breaks: lunch breaks, weekends, holidays.

Develop engaging hobbies and recreational activities.

Set aside time for reflection and spiritual development

Set aside time for reflection and meditation.

Reassess your values. What is really important in your life?

Review your goals in life. What are you working towards?

P

Emotional

Anxiety
    (Nervousness, tension, phobias, panics)
Depression
    (Sadness, lowered self-esteem, apathy and
    fatigue)
Guilt and shame
Moodiness
Loneliness
Jealously
Over-reacting
Crying

Mental

Difficulty in concentrating
Difficulty in making decisions
Difficulty 'turning off'
Frequent forgetfulness
Increased sensitivity to criticism
Negative self-critical thoughts
Distorted ideas
More rigid attitudes
Obsessional intrusive thoughts

Health

Coronary heart disease/essential
    hypertension/strokes
Stomach ulcers/colitis
Migraine/headaches
Asthma/hay fever
Skin rashes/eczema
Amenorrhoea
Diarrhoea
Irritable bowel syndrome
Back pain
Susceptibility to colds and flu

Physical

Increased heart rate (high blood pressure)
Difficulty breathing
Butterflies in the stomach
Muscle contraction (aches, pains)
Hot and cold spells (blushing, sweating)
Nausea – feeling sick
Numbness and tingling sensations
Increased blood glucose levels
Difficulty swallowing/dry mouth
Dilation of pupils
Frequent urination
Fatigue
Increased blood and urine catecholamine and
    corticosteroids
Immune system less efficient

Behavioural

Difficult sleeping/early wakening
Emotional outbursts
Irritation/anger/aggression
Excessive eating/loss of appetite
Excessive drinking and smoking
Accident proneness/trembling
Difficulty relaxing
Avoidance of particular situations
Social avoidance/withdrawal
Inactivity
Restlessness
Biting nails

Organisational

Absenteeism
Poor industrial relations
High labour turnover rates
High accident rate
Poor productivity
Job dissatisfaction

Effects of Stress

The work of **Holmes & Rahe** (1967) suggests that an accumulation of significant life events in any one year increases your vulnerability to stress related health problems. Total up your score. A score of over 300 points in one year increases your susceptibility to stress-related problems, while a score of below 150 means a relatively low amount of life change and a low susceptibility to stress-related health problems.

LIFE EVENT	LIFE CHANGE UNIT
Death of a spouse/partner	100
Divorce	73
Marital separation	65
Imprisonment	63
Death of a close family member	60
Personal injury or illness	55
Marriage	50
Moving house	49
Dismissal from work	47
Retirement	45
Change in health of family member	44
Pregnancy	40
Sexual difficulties	39
Gaining a new family member	39
Business/work changes	39
Change in financial state	38
Death of a close friend	37
Changes in amount of arguments with spouse	36
Major mortgage	32
Son or daughter leaving home	29
Outstanding personal achievement	29
Trouble with in-laws	28
Spouse begins or stops work	27
Change in living conditions	27
Change in social activities	26
Change in recreational activities	25
Change in school	24
Holidays	15
Christmas	14
Minor violation of the law	11
TOTAL SCORE	

P

❶ Stress is a positive force that improves our performance. When we are crossing a busy road we are likely to feel slightly stressed, alert, vigilant and aware of the danger and hence we cross in safety. If we were not stressed by the traffic we might be a danger to ourselves. Stress is rather like an electric current, it gives us energy but if the current is turned up too high it can produce unpleasant effects and cause a deterioration in performance.

❷ The Yerkes Dodson Law states that a certain level of stimulation or stress improves performance, but performance begins to deteriorate if stress is excessive. For example, if you are asked to separate coloured counters into different bottles under the following conditions your performance would vary as indicated on the graph.

Condition A – with no time limit or incentive.

Condition B – a financial reward related to speed and accuracy.

Condition C – a punishment of an electric shock if performance is
       poor.

Performance is likely to be best, or at its optimal level, under condition B. Under condition A there is likely not to be enough stimulation to improve performance and under condition . . . the threat of the shock puts a great deal of stress on the person causing them to get nervous and fumble. In our lives we all have to identify our optimal level of stress and be aware of being pushed past it so that our everyday performance does not deteriorate.

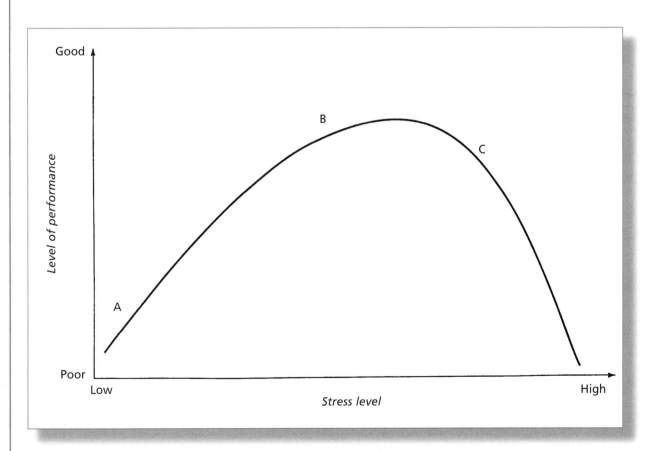

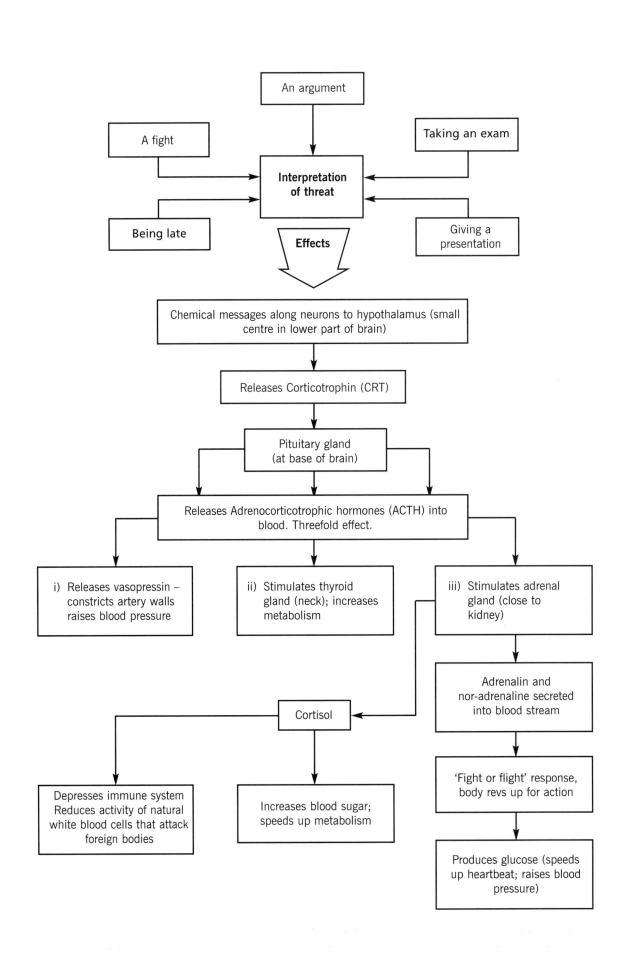

P

An unstimulating situation

Perceived demand   Perceived ability   Ability not tested.
Unstimulating

A stimulating situation

Perceived demand   Perceived ability   Ability matches demand.
Stimulating

A stressful situation

  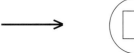

Perceived demand   Perceived ability   Demand greater than ability.
Stressful

Rethinking capabilities and demands

Initially perceived demand	Initially perceived ability	Potentially a stressful experience

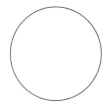 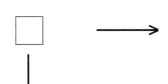 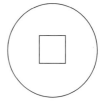

Newly perceived demand	Newly perceived ability	A stimulating experience

❶ Work stress is the single most important source of stress throughout the developed world. In one recent study of over 3,000 people 17 per cent of the sample said that they had experienced 'unpleasant emotional strain for at least half of the previous day'. In another study it is suggested that 60 per cent of absences from work are caused by stress-related disorders – the equivalent of 2–3 per cent of gross national product.

❷ With the introduction of high speed information technology and communication, combined with increased global competitiveness, rising expectations, loss of job security and reduced staff levels, experts suggest that workers have experienced significantly increased job stress over recent years.

❸ One study showed that a certain type of person could cope with high levels of stress but have low levels of illness. This type of person, labelled as stress resistant personality, had three characteristics all beginning with 'C'. These included, a sense of *control* or purpose or direction in their life; a sense of *commitment* to work, hobbies, social life and family, and a sense of *challenge* – seeing changes in life as normal and positive rather than as a threat.

❹ There are three main ways of dealing with work stress, which correspond to the sections in the following Work Stress Questionnaire. First, identify the sources of stress in your job and try to make appropriate changes – often people are not exactly sure of what the problems are but just feel demoralised, stressed or fed-up. Second, examine your strategies for coping with stress and see if they can be improved. Third, identify your symptoms of stress and attempt to manage them better.

◼ A model of work stress

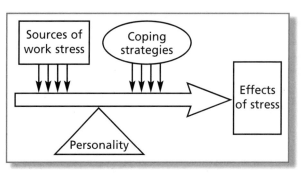

◼ Relevant factors involved in stress

Sources of work stress
Quantity/quality of work
Role issues
Level of responsibility/authority
Social/relationships
Job satisfaction
Organisational issues
Domestic effects

Coping strategies
Assertiveness
Social support
Self-organisation
Rationality
Hobbies/leisure
Self-care
Maladaptive

Effects of stress on the individual
Mental
Physical
Emotional
Behavioural

Ten unhelpful coping strategies
1 Bottle up feelings.
2 Work longer hours.
3 Don't delegate.
4 Don't say no.
5 Take work home.
6 Be a perfectionist.
7 Procrastinate and avoid.
8 Don't take breaks.
9 Don't talk about it.
10 Squeeze out hobbies.

 P

The benefits of regular exercise

'Walking is the best medicine'
– Hippocrates –

1 Exercise provides a way of releasing a great deal of muscle tension and accumulated adrenaline which is the result of high levels of stress. Exercise is a relaxant. Exercise maintains good circulation, lowers blood pressure and improves the body's immune system in its constant fight to ward off diseases.

2 Exercise improves the mood, self-image, appearance and control of weight. Exercise can be used to clear the mind of the clutter of worrying thoughts and anxiety. Hormones are released during exercise, such as endomorphines, which act as a natural anti-depressant and raise mood.

3 Ideally you should aim to do twenty to thirty minutes of exercise, two or three times a week, starting slowly and building up intensity. The best form of exercise combine the three distinct elements of *stamina, suppleness* and *strength*. Easy rhythmic movements, such as swimming, cycling and walking, are the best all-round types of exercise.

4 Your pulse rate, or heartbeat, is a good measure of your fitness. Many of the world's top athletes have a resting pulse of only forty beats per minute. In contrast a person who is out of shape may have a resting pulse of ninety to hundred beats per minute. Another indicator of a healthy heart is the speed at which your pulse rate returns to normal after vigorous exercise.

A well balanced diet

'Let food be your medicine, let medicine be your food'
– Hippocrates –

1 You would not run a classic car on low octane fuel and expect a good performance. Similarly, we cannot perform to our best on a poor diet. Healthy eating can increase our performance, strengthen our immune system and enable us to cope better with stress. Eating should be pleasurable and relaxing. Always allow time to sit down and enjoy your food. Aim to eat three main meals a day.

2 *Eat more high fibre foods*. Healthy eating does not mean eating less of everything. There is something that you can eat more of and that is fibre. The term refers to a special group of carbohydrates that you get from foods that grow in the ground. Fibre reduces the amount of cholesterol in your blood. Foods rich in fibre include: cereals, beans, vegetables, fruit, bran, wholemeal bread, pasta.

3 *Eat less fat*. Saturated fats that you find in meat, dairy products, cakes and crisps are unhealthy because they are loaded in calories which lead to weight gain. They also increase your cholesterol levels in your blood, clogging up your arteries. However, unsaturated fats do not raise cholesterol levels in the same way. These include vegetable oil and oily fish. Grill bake or boil rather than fry.

4 *Cut down on mood foods*. Certain substances such as salt, sugar, alcohol and caffeine can affect your mood. Eaten in excess these can influence your stress levels. Caffeine is a stimulate which can activate your adrenal gland and mimic the stress response. If you do drink too much caffeine your body becomes agitated and the side-effects may well be panic attacks, palpitations and headaches. Similarly, a high intake of sugar gives you a short-term surge of energy but this can lead to overworking the adrenal glands, depleting the body's strength and causing irritability and mood swings.

5 Try not to exceed the recommended weekly alcohol intake levels: 21 units for men and 14 units for women. One unit is the equivalent to one pub measure of spirits, or a glass of wine, or half a pint of beer.

6 Bear in mind the age-old adage 'Everything in moderation'.

Sources of work stress

Please place a circle around the number which best describes your work stress over the last two months.

		NO STRESS		STRESS			MUCH STRESS
1	Working long or unsociable hours.	0	1	2	3	4	5
2	Having too many different parts or roles to play.	0	1	2	3	4	5
3	Managing and supervising the work of others.	0	1	2	3	4	5
4	Clashes and conflicts with others at work.	0	1	2	3	4	5
5	Current career and promotion prospects.	0	1	2	3	4	5
6	Poor training and guidance.	0	1	2	3	4	5
7	My partner's attitude towards my work.	0	1	2	3	4	5
8	Having far too great a quantity of work to do.	0	1	2	3	4	5
9	Being unclear about what is expected of me.	0	1	2	3	4	5
10	Being responsible for managing other people.	0	1	2	3	4	5
11	My relationship with my superior/manager.	0	1	2	3	4	5
12	The job demands skills which I do not possess.	0	1	2	3	4	5
13	Poor communication and consultation in the organisation.	0	1	2	3	4	5
14	Continuing working when at home.	0	1	2	3	4	5
15	Changes and innovations in working practice.	0	1	2	3	4	5
16	Work situations creating ethical problems.	0	1	2	3	4	5
17	Having to make decisions.	0	1	2	3	4	5
18	Little encouragement and support from management.	0	1	2	3	4	5
19	Job insecurity or threat of redundancy/retirement.	0	1	2	3	4	5
20	Restricted resources and finance to work with.	0	1	2	3	4	5
21	Difficulty 'switching off' at home.	0	1	2	3	4	5
22	Having too little work to do.	0	1	2	3	4	5
23	Inadequate information about my work role.	0	1	2	3	4	5
24	Dealing with conflict and negative situations.	0	1	2	3	4	5
25	Lack of social contact with other people.	0	1	2	3	4	5
26	Wages/salary.	0	1	2	3	4	5
27	The general morale of the workforce.	0	1	2	3	4	5
28	The demands work makes on my home/personal life.	0	1	2	3	4	5
29	Amount of time spent travelling.	0	1	2	3	4	5
30	Having few clear objectives and goals to work towards.	0	1	2	3	4	5

■ Sources of work stress continued

		NO STRESS		STRESS			MUCH STRESS
31	Going to meetings/giving presentations.	0 1 2 3 4 5					
32	My relationship with others at work.	0 1 2 3 4 5					
33	Doing a job that does not stretch me.	0 1 2 3 4 5					
34	Instability and high staff turnover.	0 1 2 3 4 5					
35	Changes outside work – moving house, illness, financial, family etc.	0 1 2 3 4 5					
36	Time pressures and deadlines.	0 1 2 3 4 5					
37	Lack of variety and stimulation at work.	0 1 2 3 4 5					
38	Being responsible for managing property/money.	0 1 2 3 4 5					
39	Lack of people to talk to and share with.	0 1 2 3 4 5					
40	Feeling undervalued.	0 1 2 3 4 5					
41	Not having sufficient control, influence and power.	0 1 2 3 4 5					
42	Prioritising between work and family/home life.	0 1 2 3 4 5					
43	Fear of making a mistake.	0 1 2 3 4 5					
44	Changes in the way I have been asked to work.	0 1 2 3 4 5					
45	Work politics.	0 1 2 3 4 5					
46	Rivalry and competition from colleagues.	0 1 2 3 4 5					
47	Lack of job satisfaction and feelings of achievement.	0 1 2 3 4 5					
48	An unpleasant physical environment to work in.	0 1 2 3 4 5					
49	Changes in my personal relationships outside work.	0 1 2 3 4 5					
50	Doing work that is potentially dangerous or distressing.	0 1 2 3 4 5					
51	Little feedback about my performance.	0 1 2 3 4 5					
52	Too many different demands on my time.	0 1 2 3 4 5					
53	Socialising at informal work settings.	0 1 2 3 4 5					
54	Lack of feelings of personal development and growth.	0 1 2 3 4 5					
55	Rules and restrictions on my behaviour.	0 1 2 3 4 5					
56	Little encouragement and support from others outside work.	0 1 2 3 4 5					
Add any other sources of your job stress that are not covered:							
57		0 1 2 3 4 5					
58		0 1 2 3 4 5					

Work Stress Inventory 1

Ways of coping

Please circle the number which best describes
your way of coping over the last 2 months.

		NEVER	SOMETIMES	FREQUENT
1	Request help and support from others.	0 1 2	3 4	5
2	Talk to friends and colleagues about my worries.	0 1 2	3 4	5
3	Manage my time so that I am not rushed.	0 1 2	3 4	5
4	Remain objective, not taking things personally.	0 1 2	3 4	5
5	Enjoy hobbies and leisure activities.	0 1 2	3 4	5
6	Stay physically fit with exercise and healthy diet.	0 1 2	3 4	5
7	Avoid difficult things – put things off.	0 1 2	3 4	5
8	Delegate work when necessary.	0 1 2	3 4	5
9	Look for advice and information from superiors.	0 1 2	3 4	5
10	Work towards set goals and objectives.	0 1 2	3 4	5
11	Stand back and think things through.	0 1 2	3 4	5
12	Keep home and work separate.	0 1 2	3 4	5
13	Treat myself to something pleasurable (gifts, clothes, food).	0 1 2	3 4	5
14	Withdraw from people – bottle things up.	0 1 2	3 4	5
15	Say 'No' to extra work – refuse requests.	0 1 2	3 4	5
16	Spend time with supportive family and friends.	0 1 2	3 4	5
17	Plan ahead (days, weeks, months, years).	0 1 2	3 4	5
18	Have realistic expectations about myself, accepting my limitations.	0 1 2	3 4	5
19	Become absorbed in a rewarding or creative activity outside work.	0 1 2	3 4	5
20	Make time for periods of planned deliberate relaxation (lunchtime, evenings, weekends, holidays)	0 1 2	3 4	5
21	Work longer hours.	0 1 2	3 4	5
22	Express emotion openly and directly.	0 1 2	3 4	5
23	Confide work problems to partner.	0 1 2	3 4	5
24	Set priorities and make lists of things to do.	0 1 2	3 4	5
25	Accept situations which cannot be altered.	0 1 2	3 4	5
26	Relax and 'turn off' at home.	0 1 2	3 4	5
27	Find comfort in spiritual activity and contemplation.	0 1 2	3 4	5
28	Increase intake of alcohol, cigarettes, drugs or food.	0 1 2	3 4	5

Add any other coping strategies that you use that are not covered.

		NEVER	SOMETIMES	FREQUENT
29		0 1 2	3 4	5
30		0 1 2	3 4	5

P

Effects of stress

Please circle the number which best describes how true the statements below have been, at work or home, over the last two months.

		NOT TRUE	SOMETIMES TRUE				VERY TRUE
1	I am easily irritated and lose my temper.	0	1	2	3	4	5
2	I feel generally tired and exhausted.	0	1	2	3	4	5
3	I tend to drink, smoke, take medication or drugs more.	0	1	2	3	4	5
4	I have difficulty concentrating for any length of time.	0	1	2	3	4	5
5	I feel tense and unable to relax.	0	1	2	3	4	5
6	I have lots of aches and pains.	0	1	2	3	4	5
7	I have difficulty sleeping, or wake early.	0	1	2	3	4	5
8	I have difficulty making decisions.	0	1	2	3	4	5
9	I am generally more moody than usual.	0	1	2	3	4	5
10	I suffer from indigestion or nausea.	0	1	2	3	4	5
11	I tend to avoid difficult situations.	0	1	2	3	4	5
12	I have difficulty absorbing new information.	0	1	2	3	4	5
13	I sometimes feel panicky.	0	1	2	3	4	5
14	I suffer from frequent headaches.	0	1	2	3	4	5
15	I have noticed a definite increase/decrease in my appetite.	0	1	2	3	4	5
16	I tend to worry about many things.	0	1	2	3	4	5
17	I sometimes feel very pessimistic.	0	1	2	3	4	5
18	I sometimes feel my heart racing and feel breathless.	0	1	2	3	4	5
19	I avoid social situations and feel more withdrawn.	0	1	2	3	4	5
20	I tend to question my ability and have negative thoughts.	0	1	2	3	4	5
21	I feel generally more anxious.	0	1	2	3	4	5
22	I tend to go to the toilet quite often.	0	1	2	3	4	5
23	I have stopped doing some of the things I used to enjoy.	0	1	2	3	4	5
24	I feel less confident in doing things I used to do.	0	1	2	3	4	5
Add any other significant effects of stress you may have experienced.							
25		0	1	2	3	4	5
26		0	1	2	3	4	5

Sources of stress

(Enter scores for each question in appropriate boxes and add up factor scores)

1 ☐	2 ☐	3 ☐	4 ☐	5 ☐	6 ☐	7 ☐
8 ☐	9 ☐	10 ☐	11 ☐	12 ☐	13 ☐	14 ☐
15 ☐	16 ☐	17 ☐	18 ☐	19 ☐	20 ☐	21 ☐
22 ☐	23 ☐	24 ☐	25 ☐	26 ☐	27 ☐	28 ☐
29 ☐	30 ☐	31 ☐	32 ☐	33 ☐	34 ☐	35 ☐
36 ☐	37 ☐	38 ☐	39 ☐	40 ☐	41 ☐	42 ☐
43 ☐	44 ☐	45 ☐	46 ☐	47 ☐	48 ☐	49 ☐
50 ☐	51 ☐	52 ☐	53 ☐	54 ☐	55 ☐	56 ☐

☐	☐	☐	☐	☐	☐	☐
Quantity/ Quality	Role Issues	Responsibility Authority	Social Relationships	Job Satisfaction	Organisational Issues	Domestic Effects

Ways of coping

1 ☐	2 ☐	3 ☐	4 ☐	5 ☐	6 ☐	7 ☐
8 ☐	9 ☐	10 ☐	11 ☐	12 ☐	13 ☐	14 ☐
15 ☐	16 ☐	17 ☐	18 ☐	19 ☐	20 ☐	21 ☐
22 ☐	23 ☐	24 ☐	25 ☐	26 ☐	27 ☐	28 ☐

☐	☐	☐	☐	☐	☐	☐
Assertiveness	Social Support	Self Organisation	Rationality	Hobbies/ Leisure	Self-Care	Maladaptive

Effects of stress

1 ☐	2 ☐	3 ☐	4 ☐
5 ☐	6 ☐	7 ☐	8 ☐
9 ☐	10 ☐	11 ☐	12 ☐
13 ☐	14 ☐	15 ☐	16 ☐
17 ☐	18 ☐	19 ☐	20 ☐
21 ☐	22 ☐	23 ☐	24 ☐

☐	☐	☐	☐
Emotional	Physical	Behavioural	Mental

P

'When a man does not know what harbour he is making for, no wind is the right wind'

– Seneca –

■ The importance of goal planning

❶ Human beings are goal-directed creatures constantly striving for meaning, significance and purpose. A lack of achievable goals results in stress and tension. We all need a role, something to work towards, to give us a sense of value and control.

❷ Stress can be either the result of not having goals, having too many goals, having conflicting goals, or working towards somebody else's goals.

❸ Your goals should help you to centre your life. You need to be clear about your values, what you believe in, what is important to you, before you set goals. What kind of person do you want to be?

❹ In the study of the psychology of achievement, almost all successful people have one thing in common: they work towards set goals.

❺ Setting and working towards goals increases motivation and releases an enormous store of energy.

❻ In studies of survivors of stressful environments, such as concentration camps and prisons, those best equipped to survive were those who had or could create goals to work towards.

■ Why don't people set goals?

❶ Because they don't realise the importance of setting goals. It is amazing that given the importance of the skill of goal planning, it is a subject rarely taught in schools.

❷ People might not set goals because they don't know how to.

❸ People often don't set goals because of a deep seated 'fear of failure'. Once a goal is set, you either succeed or fail to achieve it.

■ Why goals should be written down and made specific

❶ Writing a goal down makes it visible, obvious, concrete and specific. There it is in front of you. This has the effect of waking up the unconscious and releasing energy.

❷ Writing a goal down entails a commitment. If you don't write it down, you can always say to yourself, 'I never really meant to do that anyway' and you leave your options open. Writing goals down challenges procrastination.

> **'Plan for your future because that is where you are going to spend the rest of your life'**
>
> **– Mark Twain –**

❶ Brainstorm – be creative: ecide what you really want. Brainstorm yourself by asking the question, 'What do I want out of life in the next five years?' Answer that question by writing down everything that comes into your head in terms of:

a Home/family

b Work

c Leisure and personal development

❷ Re-examine: Once you have generated these three lists go back and examine them for goals which are:

a Incompatible, for example, 'I want to be the best salesman in the company', and 'I want to spend every weekend and evening with my family'. Eliminate one or modify both goals.

b Unattainable, for example, 'I want to beat Pete Sampras at tennis'. Change this to, 'I want to win 90 per cent of my club tournament matches this summer'.

❸ Rewrite in terms of outcome: Write out your modified goals in clear specific language in terms of an outcome, for example, 'By next Christmas I will have written and had typed up a five-thousand word short story.'

❹ Create action plans: Write an action plan or a series of specific activities for the accomplishment of that goal. These are the steps that need to be taken to achieve that goal; again they should be specific. Try to aim for at least six activities for each goal. For example, for writing the short story, activities might be:

a Buy a word processor

b Enrolling on a course for creative writing

c Buying a book on creative writing

d Setting aside Tuesday evening for writing

e Arrange to meet Jim and show him the first draft on Sunday 6 September

f Set up a desk in the spare room

❺ Identity obstacles: There will be obstacles to overcome. Identify and plan for these and take the view that obstacles come to instruct. For example, obstacle: 'I might have to work late on a Tuesday'; solution: 'Alter the sales meeting to Wednesday so it will be easier to get away earlier on Tuesday.'

❻ Build in rewards: Work out a reward system, for example, 'If I've completed the story by Christmas I will buy myself a compact disc player.'

❼ Visualise the end result: Have a clear mental image of what things will be like when you achieve your goal. This acts as a motivator and helps you release energy.

P

The following exercise is a useful way to loosen up your thinking, help you identify core values and put you in a positive frame of mind for goal planning. Each question should be answered quickly in the allotted time.

What are the five basic values in life that are most important to you (eg, friendship, health, etc)?
(Take 60 seconds)

What are your three most important long-term life goals?
(30 seconds)

What would you do if you had six months to live?
(30 seconds)

How would you change your life if you become an instant millionaire?
(30 seconds)

What activities give you the greatest feeling of importance and satisfaction?
(60 seconds)

What would you like people to say about you at your funeral?
(30 seconds)

What have you always wanted to do but been afraid to attempt?
(30 seconds)

Goal Planning Sheet

1 BRAINSTORM

(Write down as many goals as come to mind, perhaps separating the areas of home, work, leisure, relationships)

Home	Work	Leisure	Relationships
◆ ◆ ◆	◆ ◆ ◆	◆ ◆ ◆	◆ ◆ ◆

2 REWRITE THREE GOALS WITH SPECIFIC, TIMED OUTCOME
(eliminate or modify unrealistic goals)

i.

ii.

iii.

3 IDENTIFY STEPS NECESSARY TO ACHIEVE GOALS

◆ ◆ ◆

◆ ◆ ◆

◆ ◆ ◆

4 POTENTIAL OBSTACLES

◆ ◆ ◆

◆ ◆ ◆

◆ ◆ ◆

P

'Time is the scarcest of resources and unless it can be managed nothing else can be managed'

– Peter Drucker –

Time is the most scarce and valuable resource we have. If we do not manage our time successfully we can feel frustrated, dissatisfied and stressed. The central principle of time management is that it is important for all of us to spend our time doing those things that we value.

❶ Know your goals in life: Identify the values, activities and goals that are most important in your life. These goals are the map by which you give direction to your life and schedule your time. These large overall goals can be broken down into smaller manageable tasks to accomplish (the salami principle).

❷ Rank priorities: Activities can be ranked in terms of what is important and what is less important. The Italian economist Pareto gave his name to the Pareto Principle or the 80/20 rule. Twenty per cent of your efforts will bring 80 per cent of your rewards, while the other 80 per cent of your effort will bring only 20 per cent of your rewards. Pareto suggested we recognise and prioritise the 20 per cent. Ask yourself, 'How important is this to me?

❸ Plan and write it down: There is a misconception that planning adds time to a task. Minutes spent in planning will be saved many times over. Use a calender, diary, and 'to do' lists. 'When you are feeling listless make a list'. A written plan gives us the ability to stand back and develop 'helicopter vision'.

❹ Delegate tasks: One of the biggest causes of stress is the notion that we have to do everything by ourselves. Take a look at your schedule and decide what can be handed on to somebody else.

❺ Work out a system: Muddle makes unnecessary work, wastes time and creates frustration. Spend time organising your environment so that you have 'a place for everything and everything in its place'. Establish a regular routine, carving out protected time for high priority activities.

❻ Don't procrastinate: By putting off today's tasks until tomorrow you are simply storing up work for yourself. Set yourself deadlines, use them to increase motivation, and maybe add inbuilt rewards.

❼ Leave slack in your timetable: Never fill up your timetable completely, always allow a little slack or leeway. Then if something crops up, you are not overwhelmed.

❽ Learn to say 'no': If we cannot 'turn off the tap' of demands and requests of others we simply have no control over our lives. We will end up being the servant to the priorities of others, constantly deflected from what we really want to do.

❾ One thing at a time: We may have many things to do but we cannot do them all at the same time. Important tasks usually require our whole concentration and energy. This is not to say that you cannot double up at times, by for example doing the ironing and watching television.

❿ Identify prime time: Identify when you work best and plan that time for your most demanding tasks. For most people it is early in the morning, with performance tailing off by lunchtime. Similarly allocate undemanding tasks to times when your energy levels may be low.

⓫ Overcome perfectionism: If you have to get everything absolutely right you will find it difficult to vary your speed according to priorities. The perfectionist often becomes bogged down in small details, missing out on the broader picture. Dare to be average sometimes!

⓬ Keep a balance: Vary and contrast activities in different areas of your life, spending time in a balance between work, home, leisure, physical activity and mental activity. Plan natural breaks during the day, relax at weekends and take holidays.

Time Management

'Don't Do. Delegate'

■ Delegation

Delegation means getting things done, or achieving goals, through the efforts of other people. It is the major skill of management, whether you are managing an office, a business or a home. It means giving people authority to do interesting things, not just passing on all the unpleasant jobs to somebody else.

The underlying principle is that any advancement or progress depends on producing results beyond our own capabilities – we will never make progress if we have to do everything ourselves. Lack of the ability to delegate means holding on to the idea, 'I'll do it all myself'. This often leads to the person feeling under pressure, working longer hours, lacking time and feeling isolated. Poor delegation often means that others do not develop skills and there is poor team spirit.

■ Benefits of delegation

Delegation gives you:

❶ more time,

❷ increases your productivity,

❸ frees you from the web of petty detail,

❹ forces you to plan and organise,

❺ increases your job satisfaction, and promotes variety,

❻ helps others take on responsibility, develop initiative and learn new skills,

❼ promotes team spirit.

■ Fears or obstacles stop people delegating

There are a number of reasons why people find it difficult to delegate. Most of these are underlying, often unrecognised, fears and insecurities.

Guilt: 'I can't ask Jane to do it she, she already has her hands full', 'I don't want to appear idle', 'I donlt want to appear idle'.

Fear of failure: 'What if Pete really blows it – that will look bad for me.'

Fear of success or envy: 'What if he succeeds too well? They might think he is better at this job than me. I will feel redundant.'

Fear of Letting Go: The martyr syndrome. 'I'll do it myself and feel virtuous – nobody ever helps me', 'I can do it better myself', 'I want credit for the result.'

■ How to delegate effectively

❶ **Give clear instructions and information.** This does not mean telling the person exactly how to do something, but it does mean outlining what needs to be done, explaining why it needs doing, and setting standards and deadlines.

❷ **Pass on responsibility and authority.** Delegate the entire task to one person, not half a task. Provide the person with the resources to do the job and stay in contact and provide back up.

❸ **Check if the person understands what is required.** Make sure that the person has adequate skills to carry out the task. Check also how they feel about doing the task.

❹ **Monitor progress, arrange for regular updates.** Provide supervision and support, but do not keep looking over the person's shoulder. Praise in public; if you have to criticise, do so in private.

❺ **Allow for as much autonomy or creativity as you can.** Give the person latitude to make decisions.

❻ **Give feedback and praise.** When the task is completed go over it with the person, giving specific comments and praise, so that the person can learn from it.

P

Possible causes and solutions of poor delegation

POSSIBLE CAUSES	IS IT ME?	POSSIBLE SOLUTIONS
What if she does it better than me? I will then be dispensable.		Be grateful. Nobody can be equally good at everything.
She already has too much to do. I do not want to overload her.		Have an overview of what are her priorities.
What if she fails? It will make me look bad.		Train her, pass on skills. Learn from mistakes.
I could do the job better myself.		Don't try to be a perfectionist; let things go.
I do not want to appear either as a tyrant or lazy.		Explain the reasons why you are delegating.
The other person might refuse.		You can ask and she can refuse.
I like doing the task. I prefer 'doing things' than 'managing'.		That's fine but what are the effects on your limited time.
It would be quicker to do it myself.		It might be in the short term – but consider the longer term.
I'll do it myself as usual. I can feel good, virtuous, martyrish.		Resentment can build up. You instill guilt in others

IDENTIFY CAUSES FOR YOUR POOR DELEGATION	IDENTIFY POSSIBLE CHALLENGES OR SOLUTIONS
1	
2	
3	
4	

'Procrastination is the thief of time'

– Edward Young

Procrastination means putting off something that we know we need to do. Most of us procrastinate to some extent. We have all said, 'I'll do it later', or 'I must get around to doing that'. But some people habitually procrastinate to such an extent that tasks build up and their lives become very stressful.

Procrastination often amounts to deliberately avoiding having to confront our fears. Procrastination flourishes in two optimal conditions. First, when the task is not urgent – we do not have to do it right now – there is time to do it in the future. Second, when there is something more pleasurable to do now. Procrastination is usually about putting pleasure before pain.

■ Seven reasons why people procrastinate

1 **Lacking a sense of mastery.** You may hold the attitude that successful people achieve their goals without frustration and self doubt. When the going gets tough you think – 'this is not how it should be, this is wrong' and give up. Whereas people who are consistently successful have a 'sense of mastery' and asume that life will be a tough frustrating struggle, to be mastered. So, when they encounter obstacles they just carry on because that's what they expect.

2 **Assume you have to be in the mood.** Procrastinators often think, 'I don't feel like it, I'll wait until I'm in the mood'. But with some tasks that are boring or too demanding you will never feel in the mood. Successful people will often put action before motivation. Once you get started and begin to feel a sense of accomplishment it spurs you on to do more.

3 **Fear of failure**. You may leave the task until the last minute and then say, 'I didn't have enough time to do it properly'. By doing so you give yourself an excuse and protect yourself from the reality that your best effort might not have been good enough. Alternatively, if you are something of a perfectionist, you may think, 'I do not want to start unless I can do it properly (perfectly) – otherwise I will feel like a failure'.

4 **Fear of rejection or intimacy**. You may avoid inviting friends around, or making that telephone call, in case you get rejected. Alternatively you may not feel comfortable with the other person getting to know you. Procrastination helps you maintain a safe emotional distance, allowing you to avoid revealing yourself to others.

5 **Fear of success.** If you do it really well you may draw attention to yourself or create more work for yourself.

6 **Getting back at somebody.** You may put something off as a way of getting back at somebody. If you are feeling bossed around or coerced into doing something, your procrastination may be an indirect way of expressing anger or rebelling.

7 **Lack of commitment.** You may simply not consider the task important enough to put in the effort. Alternatively, you may think, 'It's an unpleasant task and I would prefer to do something else'.

 P

1 **List the advantages and disadvantages of procrastinating from the task.** Draw up two columns on a sheet of paper and list the advantages and disadvantages. Remember, procrastination has many advantages: it's easy, you don't have to face the possibility of failure, you can do something else more pleasurable. It is important to recognise the advantages, as they may be too good to give up. Weigh the advantages against the disadvantages. You may learn that the task is just not right for you (see Exercise).

2 **Just do it.** Your expectations are usually worse than reality. Like getting into the cold swimming pool, it is better to just jump in.

3 **Plan it.** Put it in your diary, or on your 'to do' list. Make it part of your routine rather than having to think about it. Start the day with your least pleasant task, then the day gets better. Decide on a specific time to get started.

4 **Break the task up into smaller parts.** If the task is overwhelming, do it a piece at a time. For example, just plan to do 15 minutes worth of work, often the sense of achievement will motivate you to do more. Mix the task up with more pleasable activities and carry it out little and often.

5 **Think differently.** Challenge distorted thinking such as 'awfulising', 'black and white thinking', and 'jumping to conclusions'. Concentrate on how good you will feel when you have done it. Lower your expectations. Aim to do an adequate, rather than a brilliant, job.

6 **Plan rewards and reinforcements**. Reward yourself something once you have done the dreaded deed. If it doesn't work out as well as you hoped, view the experience as valuable learning.

7 **Set deadlines and work towards them.** Say to yourself, 'I will have this done before the end of the week, or the end of the year'.

■ Exercise

What do you procrastinate over? Write out a list of the tasks that you put off, from your home, work, and personal life. Select one of those tasks and write down a list of the things you say to yourself when you are putting it off. See how your reasons correspond to the list above. Using the strategies above try to carry that task out now.

Write down what you're putting off _____

Write down the advantages and disadvantages of putting it off

Advantages	Disadvantages
1	1
2	2
3	3
4	4
5	5
6	6

Introduction

Modern society has changed dramatically over the last two decades. The speed of life has increased, with more rapid transport, instant communications and even fast food. As the pace of life has increased there has also been an increase in certain stress related illnesses such as coronary heart disease and strokes.

We all have different temperaments, but for certain people life is a constant rush, a hurry from one activity or achievement to another. This style of behaviour often has its roots in early childhood where the 'need to achieve' and be successful is instilled from an early age.

The combination of this type of temperament and the increased pace of modern life can often lead to major stress problems or 'hurry sickness'.

What is Type A behaviour?

Two American cardiologists, Friedman and Rosenman, noticed that a great many of the people they saw with coronary heart disease and strokes tended to be of a similar nature, and were likely to be rather difficult to rehabilitate, as they did not find it easy to adjust their lifestyles. They initiated research into what has come to be known as Type A behaviour.

Type A behaviour is characterised by a cluster of traits:

❶ *Competitiveness:* An overriding need to achieve;

❷ *Hurry sickness:* An intense sense of time urgency;

❸ *Hostility:* Inappropriate aggression if progress is impeded;

❹ *Joyless striving:* always on the go, with many projects at once;

❺ *Inability to relax:* difficulty turning off.

Type B behaviour is, on the other hand, the exact opposite, the individual being characterised by being more relaxed, less hurried and less inclined to compete.

Type A behaviour and your health

A number of research studies have indicated that individuals who score highly on Type A behaviour have double the risk of heart disease compared with those who are classified as having low Type A scores or Type B behaviour. This is independent of other traditional risk factors such as blood pressure, serum cholesterol, smoking and age. Type A behaviour is also associated with other stress-related conditions such as stomach ulcers, allergies, the exaggerated response of the sympathetic nervous system to stress ('fight or flight' response) and poor levels of mental health (anxiety and depression). Type A behaviour also seems to be linked with high levels of success in career and financial terms.

Physiology of Type A behaviour

The underlying physiology of Type A behaviour seems to be that such behaviour leads to excessive discharge of the stress hormones – noradrenaline, adrenaline and cortisol – and one result is an excess of insulin in the bloodstream. This can mean that it can take three or four times longer than normal to get rid of dietary cholesterol after meals. A potential result is a narrowing of blood vessels, together with increased deposits of clotting elements in the blood.

Research indicates that, with the right intervention, people can manage their Type A behaviour effectively, reducing the risks of physical and mental ill-health without impairing their performance.

P

Identify your Type A behaviour on a check list and then make deliberate attempts to 'go against the grain' and alter that behaviour by the following methods:

1 **Slow down:** Be aware of your obsessional time-directed lifestyle and try to slow down. Deliberately walk or eat slowly, setting aside a specific time period where you have to stay at the dinner table. Try to schedule fewer activities each day.

2 **Take breaks:** Build into your daily and weekly timetable stress-free 'breathing spaces' where you deliberately try to relax. This might be a five-minute period when you carry out a muscle relaxation exercise or breathing exercise, a walk in the park at lunchtime, or a break where you read the newspaper. Plan regular holidays and if possible get away to a different environment.

3 **Commit yourself to hobbies:** As part of an effort to broaden yourself and reduce obsessional time-directed behaviour, deliberately develop leisure activities and hobbies, for example, sailing, gardening, walking or sewing. Commit yourself fully to these activities. Try to engage in uncompetitive trivial activities just for fun.

4 **Express feelings:** Try to adopt a more positive approach to expressing yourself and how you feel. Take time to thank others and show appreciation when somebody has done something for you. Talk to others about how you are feeling – ventilate feelings rather than bottling them up.

5 **Practice listening:** Search out somebody who talks slowly and deliberately. Have a slow conversation. Try to hold back from making yourself the centre of attention. Ask yourself 'Do I really have anything important to say?'.

6 **Forget time:** Give yourself occasional breaks where you remove your watch and try to loose your sense of time. Break the habit of always being punctual – deliberately miss a few deadlines or turn up for a meeting five minutes late.

7 **Manage your hostility:** Identify the triggers – keep a diary. Challenge your rigid thinking, particularly the tendency to use the words 'should', 'must' and 'ought'. Loosen up those thoughts, replace 'should' with 'it would be nice if'. Try occasionally to say to yourself 'it doesn't matter'.

8 **Learn to relax:** Learn a relaxation technique and try to practice once a day.

9 **Have a chat:** Make a point of chatting or engaging in small talk or a conversation that has no specific purpose. Slow down. Idle the time away. Try to laugh or make somebody laugh.

10 **Understand the reasons:** Take time out to assess the cause of your Type A behaviour. Did your parents' approval depend on how successful and achieving you were as a child. Ask yourself, 'What am I trying to prove?' Does your idealism and striving improve or diminish the quality of your life?

Circle the number that you feel most closely represents your own behaviour in your everyday life. Then add up your score. Try to reduce your score by deliberately changing your behaviour.

Type A Behaviour Questionnaire

Casual about appointments	0 1 2 3 4 5 6 7 8 9 10	Never late
Not competitive	0 1 2 3 4 5 6 7 8 9 10	Very competitive
Impatient while waiting	10 9 8 7 6 5 4 3 2 1 0	Can wait patiently
Never feel rushed	0 1 2 3 4 5 6 7 8 9 10	Always rushed
Emphatic in speech (fast, forceful)	10 9 8 7 6 5 4 3 2 1 0	Slow deliberate talker
Care about satisfying self irrespective of what others think	0 1 2 3 4 5 6 7 8 9 10	Want good job recognised by others
Slow doing things (eating, walking etc)	0 1 2 3 4 5 6 7 8 9 10	Fast doing things (eating, walking etc)
Hard driving (pushing yourself and others)	10 9 8 7 6 5 4 3 2 1 0	Easy going
Express feelings	0 1 2 3 4 5 6 7 8 9 10	Hide feelings
Many outside interests	0 1 2 3 4 5 6 7 8 9 10	Few interests outside home/work
Ambitious	10 9 8 7 6 5 4 3 2 1 0	Unambitious
Take things one at a time	0 1 2 3 4 5 6 7 8 9 10	Try to do many things at once; think about what you will do next
Eager to get things done	10 9 8 7 6 5 4 3 2 1 0	Casual
Good listener	0 1 2 3 4 5 6 7 8 9 10	Anticipate what others are going to say – finish sentences, nod, interrupt

Scoring

Below 70 Tending towards Type B
0–100 Moderate Type A
Over 100 High-scoring Type A

(adapted from **Bortner RW & Rosenman RH,** 'The Measurement of Pattern – A Behaviour', *Journal of Chronic Disorders* 20, pp 525–33, 1967.)

128   © T Powell 2000 – This page may be photocopied for instructional use only.   **P**

'Problems are opportunities in work clothes'

– Henry Kaiser –

■ Introduction

Problem solving is a simple but effective technique. We may do it naturally but it is often useful to deliberately go through the stages of finding a solution in a methodical fashion. Don't be put off by its simplicity.

a Take one problem at a time

b Don't waste time on problems that cannot be solved.

❶ Identify and define clearly what the problem is

The problem could appear in any area of your life and could range from deciding where to go on holiday, how to get up earlier in the morning, or how to get a new job. The important part of this stage is working out exactly what the problem is, moving from very general feelings to specific, concrete problems and questions.

Example: Where to go on holiday in the summer.

❷ Brainstorm

This means spending time generating a list of as many possible options as you can. Don't think about whether they are realistic or not. In brainstorming sessions everything goes; the only rule is that you cannot criticise or laugh at a suggested option – be as creative and imaginative as possible.

a Package holiday to Spain.
b Caravan in Lake District.
c Friends' cottage in Wales.
d Visit sister in Australia.
e Camping in the New Forest.
f Chalet at seaside (Britain).

❸ Decide which options are realistic and unrealistic

Consider the consequences of each course of action and decide which options are realistic and unrealistic eliminate unrealistic options.

a Too expensive.
b Caravan too small with baby.
c Possible.
d Too expensive.
e Possible but difficult with baby.
f Possible.

❹ Choose the option that is both most rewarding and feasible

Look at the pros and cons of the remaining options and decide which is the most viable. A useful strategy at this stage is the two column technique. Write down the advantages and disadvantages of each option.

c Friends' cottage in Wales: Pros – not too expensive, plenty of room, only one hour's drive from coastal beaches, best of both worlds, baby would be fine. Cons – weather might be foul, area is not as interesting as the Lake District or New Forest.

❺ Prepare and plan strategies for the accomplishment of chosen option

Once the option has been chosen, it then becomes a matter of planning how to achieve that goal. Objectives or stepping stones on the way to achieving it must be identified. Obstacles also need to be considered.

a Contact friends to see if it is vacant.
b Arrange to have time off work.
c Find out school summer holidays.
d Get information and map of the area.

Then try it out and evaluate what happens.

The Five Stages of Problem Solving

SECTION 5 – CHANGING HABITS & BEHAVIOUR

CHANGING HABITS & BEHAVIOUR

■ Books for Professionals

Bennett G (ed), *Treating Drug Abusers,* Tavistock/Routledge, London, 1989.

Fordyce WE, *Behavioural Methods for Chronic Pain and Illness*, Mosby, St Louis, Missouri, 1976.

Garner DM & Garfinkel PE, *Handbook of Psychotherapy for Anorexia Nervosa and Bulimia*, Guildford Press, New York, 1985.

Hawton K, *Sex Therapy: A Practical Guide*, Oxford Medical Publications, Oxford, 1985.

Masters WH & Johnson VE, *Human Sexual Inadequacy*, Little Brown, Boston, 1970.

Orford J, *Excessive Appetites: A Psychological View of Addictions*, Wiley, New York, 1985.

Williams E & Barlow R, *Anger Control Training*, Winslow Press, Bicester, 1998.

■ Books for Clients

Argyle M & Henderson M, *The Anatomy of Relationships and the Rules and Skills Needed to Manage Them Successfully,* Heinemann, London, 1983.

Broome A & Jellicoe ?, *A Self Help Guide to Managing Pain*, Methuen/British Psychology Society, 1987.

Chalder T, *Coping with Chronic Fatigue*, Sheldon Press, London, 1995.

Colclough B, *Tomorrow I'll Be Different: The Effective Way to Stop Drinking*, Viking, London, 1993.

Cooper PJ, *Bulimia Nervosa: A Guide to Recovery*, London, Robinson, 1993.

Fairburn C, *Overcoming Binge Eating*, Guildford Press, New York, 1995.

Orbach S, *Fat is a Feminist Issue*, Vols. 1 & 2, Hamlyn, London, 1978.

Robertson I & Healher N, *Let's Drink to Your Health – A Self-Help Guide to Sensible Drinking*, British Psychological Society, Leicester, 1986.

■ Addresses

Action on Smoking and Health (ASH), 102 Clifton Street, London EC2A 4HW.
Tel 020 7739 5902

Alcoholics Anonymous, PO Box 514, 11 Redcliffe Gardens, London SW10 9BQ.
(Local addresses in telephone directory.)

Relate (The National Marriage Guidance Council), Herbert Grey College, Little Church Street, Rugby CV21 3AP.
Tel 01788 573241

'Habit is either the best of servants or the worst of masters'
– Nathaniel Emmons –

❶ Habits are learned: Disorders of habit can range from nail biting and spasms to eating disorders, problems with alcohol, drug misuse, smoking and gambling. The one thing they all have in common is that they are learned behaviours with short-term rewards and long-term costs. As they are learned, they can be unlearned.

❷ Motivation: The most important step towards breaking a habit is deciding that you want to change. Motivation to change goes through a cycle of different stages. The stages of this cycle consist of: thinking about changing, making a decision to change, acting on that decision, maintaining that action, then either relapsing or exiting from the cycle and then breaking the habit.

❸ Self monitoring: The next step is to carry out an accurate assessment of the problem by the process of self-monitoring or keeping a diary sheet. When does it happen? How? What are the antecedents? What are the consequences? What thoughts and emotions are associated with the habit? This self-assessment can lead to greater understanding, greater control and a baseline measure of frequency and severity.

❹ Alter antecedents and consequences: You can work out an intervention plan based on information from the self-monitoring assessment. It might consist of:

Altering antecedents or what occurs before the habit. Assessment often shows that the habit is related to a particular situation or emotional state, for example hours of boredom, feeling anxious or being in a particular situation.

Altering consequences. At the moment your habit is being maintained by certain short-term consequences or 'pay-offs' – these need to be altered. Introduce a system of rewards and incentives to deliberately change the pay-offs.

❺ Set goals to reduce frequency: Set yourself reduction targets and goals. If you smoke 10 cigarettes a day on average, set a goal of eight cigarettes.

❻ Develop intervention strategies: Establish a repertoire of coping strategies which can be implemented when you are feeling particularly vulnerable to resorting to the behaviour.

Draw up a list of activities that are incompatible with the habit and distract you from the urge. For example, eating fruit instead of chocolate, or chewing gum instead of smoking, going for a bike ride instead of bingeing etc.

❼ Challenge negative thoughts: Work out a list of positive thoughts that you can say to yourself when feeling vulnerable. For example, 'I don't need a cigarette but I'd like one', 'If I can resist for the next hour the urge will reduce'.

❽ Massed practice: If the habit is something that is out of voluntary control, like a 'twitch', set aside time for repeated practice; deliberately carry out the habit for a limited period of, say, 10 minutes; this has the effect of increasing your feeling of control.

❾ Accept setbacks: Don't be discouraged if you relapse. Relapses are a natural part of progress. Learn from them.

Breaking a Habit

'Habit is habit and is not to be flung out of the window, but to be coaxed downstairs, a step at a time'

– Mark Twain –

How to Give up Smoking

❶ Make a definite decision to stop smoking. Write down the reasons why you want to stop and display them in a prominent place. Start with:

a Every cigarette smoked shortens a person's life by five minutes.
b Smoking causes cancer, strokes, heart disease and bronchitis.

❷ For one week keep a daily smoking record chart showing the number of cigarettes smoked each day and exactly where you smoked each cigarette.

❸ Aim to reduce gradually. Calculate the average number smoked each day; this is your baseline to work from. Divide your average daily total by six and then subtract that figure from the daily total, which is your goal to work towards next week. Example: Baseline average = 24. 24 divided by 6 = 4. Next week's target is 24 – 4 = 20. So next week you can only smoke 20 cigarettes a day.

❹ Eliminate the easiest cigarette first. Identify cigarettes with particular times of the day or activities. For example, the coffee cigarette, the driving cigarette, the after-lunch cigarette, the drinking cigarette. Devise a strategy for overcoming each cigarette. For example, break the habit of drinking coffee – have tea instead and have a biscuit.

❺ Challenge and dispute thoughts associated with smoking. For example, replace: 'It would be nice to have a cigarette right now' with: 'I don't need to have a cigarette right now – I have a choice. If I break this habit my health will improve, I'm likely to live longer, I'll save money and I won't be polluting the atmosphere for others'. Challenging thoughts of continuing to smoke is the key to breaking the habit.

❻ Collect cigarette stubs in a small bottle (about 2 inches in height) with a cap on it. As the weeks go by, the odour from the bottle will become increasingly unpleasant. Remove the cap and take a sniff if you feel an overwhelming urge to smoke.

❼ Set aside any money you have saved from not smoking and buy yourself something special.

❽ When you do smoke, smoke rapidly. Do not inhale and only smoke half the cigarette.

❾ Break as many habits in the chain of smoking as possible. Change your brand. Buy your cigarettes from a different shop. Keep your cigarettes in a different place (preferably where they are more difficult to reach). Think to yourself, 'One hour at a time', when deliberately trying to abstain.

❿ When you have broken the habit, always call yourself a non-smoker, not an ex-smoker. Say, 'I don't smoke' not, 'I've given up'.

P

Introduction

Bulimia is characterised by seriously disturbed eating habits which can include; regular food binges, vomiting and purging episodes, strict dieting and fasting, and misuse of laxatives and diuretics – all in an attempt to control body weight and shape. There is usually an extreme fear of 'fatness'. The full clinical condition occurs in 1 per cent of young women in Western society, although between 5–10 per cent of young women are prone to binge eating. It rarely occurs in men.

The person with bulimia is engaged in a constant battle with food – a love-hate relationship exists. Eating habits are chaotic with no regularity. Many are consumed by a powerful desire to be thin and are elated if they find that they have lost weight and depressed if they find that they have gained weight. People with bulimia often have a disturbance in body image. They tend to over-estimate their own size and feel that their bodies are larger than they actually are. On top of this they have a realistically small ideal size.

What causes Bulimia Nervosa?

There seem to be a number of predisposing factors, but perhaps the most consistent one is low self-esteem. Often, early family life is characterised by some unhappiness. Prior to the development of bulimia one third of patients have suffered from depression themselves, one third previously had anorexia and there is evidence that suggests that one third have been sexually abused. There is also strong evidence that the person with bulimia often tends to have a higher than average natural weight. Their personality turns towards perfectionism and they set high standards for themselves. Bulimia is heavily influenced by social and cultural factors. The most significant precipitating factor is usually a period of dieting which has been unsuccessful.

A number of psychological factors serve to perpetuate bulimia nervosa which are illustrated in the diagram below. A number of vicious circles are created where low self-esteem leads to concerns about shape and weight, which leads to strict dieting, which results in binge eating, which results in self-induced vomiting, which results in increased low self-esteem, increased preoccupation with shape and weight, more bingeing, and so the vicious circle continues.

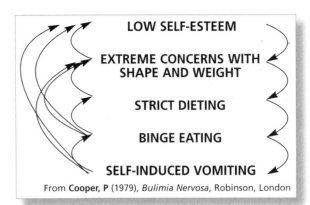

From **Cooper, P** (1979), *Bulimia Nervosa*, Robinson, London

Why can't I just stop bingeing?

The answer is that you probably unwittingly adopt a method of coping which is counter-productive. For example, fasting after a binge may make you feel better, but it also significantly increases your chances of bingeing again. Similarly, vomiting is a trap which leads to more eating, which in turn leads to more vomiting. Dieting is rarely successful. There is good evidence that dieting places people under such physical and psychological pressure to eat that it paradoxically causes people to overeat. In order to overcome bulimia you must give up the idea of dieting. The vast majority of people who give up a pattern of dieting and bingeing and replace it with a pattern of regular eating do not gain weight.

Weight

The only way to find out what your normal weight should be is to reinstate normal eating habits and see over a period of months what your weight should be. The ultimate choice is often, 'Is being a few pounds over what you are entirely happy with a worthwhile price to pay for normal eating habits and a normal lifestyle?'

Treatment

Research suggests that anti-depressant medication can help initially reduce the frequency of binges, but the person usually does not stop bingeing altogether or dieting and as such the results do not last. Cognitive-behavioural therapy, with the focus on changing behavioural patterns and challenging and changing thoughts and beliefs, has been shown to be the most effective treatment.

❶ **Monitor your eating:** Keep a record of everything you eat and when you eat it. Also record when you engage in bingeing or vomiting. On your diary sheet also keep a record of your thoughts and feelings. Examine your diary sheet and see if there is a particular pattern or triggers.

❷ **Institute a meal plan:** The next stage involves gradually learning to eat regularly and more specifically. It means attempting to eat three meals a day with two or three snacks. Your immediate reaction might be that this is a recipe for weight gain but this is actually not the case. Eating regular meals does not make you fat. Decide on certain times for eating and make an effort to stick to those times. For example breakfast 7.30 am, snack 10.00 am, lunch 1.00 pm, snack 4.30 pm, supper 7.30 pm, snack 10.30 pm. The idea of eating regularly is to displace the tendency to binge, so the time between episodes of planned eating is quite short, only 3 to 4 hours. Plan the content of meals ahead of time.

❸ **Learning to intervene and prevent bingeing:**

a Enlist support. It is often very helpful to enlist the help of a close friend or relative to help you out with this programme.

b Prepare a list of alternative activities that might be useful to implement if you feel things are going wrong or you have the urge to binge. It is helpful if these activities require physical activity, the use of your hands, they are away from your habitual eating place such as the kitchen, they are pleasurable and 'easily do-able'. A list might include; phoning a friend, going for a walk or a bike ride, playing a musical instrument, doing the garden, having a bath etc.

c Restrict eating to one or two specified areas within the house, such as the kitchen or dining room.

d Eat slowly and do not engage in any other activities while eating such as reading or watching television.

e Before eating plan exactly what you are going to do when you have finished your meal.

f Limit the amount of bingeable food in the house. Do not leave leftovers around. Always put food away. Buy small quantities of food. Never eat directly from containers, always place food on a plate.

g When shopping for food prepare a list of what you are going to buy. Do not shop when you are hungry or when you are vulnerable to binge.

h Do not let other people bully you into eating food you do not want. Practice saying 'No, thank you'.

❹ **Problem solving:** It is important for people with bulimia nervosa to recognise that often they use food as a way of solving problems which overwhelm them. The person with bulimia needs to ask themselves the question, 'Why do I have an urge to over-eat now? What is the problem that lies behind the feeling?' Try and write down what you think the problem is. What is going through your head?

❺ **Changing beliefs and thoughts:** Reconsider the link between self-esteem and body weight and shape. Make a list of personal attributes you consider valuable in others and then yourself. How high does size and weight come? Challenge 'perfectionism' and 'all or nothing thinking'.

❻ **Eliminate dieting:** When you reach this stage it is likely that your control is precarious, as you are only eating small quantities of low calorie food. Consider which foods and situations you avoid because you consider them to be 'dangerous' and institute a programme for gradual re-introduction. Like treating any phobia draw up a hierarchy and starting with the easiest begin to confront them.

❼ **Expect a relapse:** Everybody will relapse. Do not blame yourself, but try to understand what has happened and learn from it. Do not abandon your programme.

 P

Physical effects of binge eating

◆ Abdominal distension. This follows binge eating and is often accompanied by breathlessness due to the diaphragm being pushed up by the bloated stomach.

◆ Menstrual disturbances – risk of infertility.

◆ General digestive problems such as stomach cramps, wind, constipation and diarrhoea.

◆ Rupture of the stomach. This is rare but can happen in people who avoid eating for a period of some days and then have a gross binge.

Physical effects of self-induced vomiting

◆ Swelling of the glands around the face. The salivary glands and parotid glands around the jaw become enlarged. The swelling gives the face a rounded appearance which the bulimic often misinterprets as evidence of general fatness.

◆ Damage to throat, hoarseness of the voice and recurrent throat infections.

◆ Erosion of tooth enamel.

◆ Bursting of blood vessels around the eye.

◆ Damage to sphincter muscles at the entrance of the stomach.

Physical effects of misusing laxatives and diuretics

◆ Damage to the muscles lining the bowels.

◆ Chronic diarrhoea and malabsorption.

◆ Fluid and body salt abnormalities.

◆ Laxatives have little impact on calorie absorption and diuretics have none at all.

Physical effects of either self-induced vomiting and/or purgative abuse

◆ Loss of body potassium which can lead to fatal heart irregularities, episodes of palpitations and kidney failure.

◆ Dehydration, resulting in dry mouth, extreme thirst, constipation and dry skin.

◆ Other metabolic disturbances may produce profound weakness, pins and needles in the hands and legs, muscle twitches and cramps.

Effect of dieting

◆ Repeatedly going on and off diets usually causes weight gain over time, because the bodies metabolism alters. When the person stops dieting and starts eating normally, metabolic efficiency persists and they gain weight rapidly.

Effect on psychological state

◆ Secret and lonely existence

◆ Shame, guilt and depression.

◆ Impaired personal relationships and social life.

◆ Poor concentration.

Physical Effects of Bulimia Nervosa

Eating Diary Sheet

DATE:

DAY:

MEAL PLAN:

TIME	FOOD AND LIQUID CONSUMED	PLACE	BINGEING/ PURGING EPISODES	THOUGHTS & FEELINGS SURROUNDING OVEREATING

P

What is anorexia nervosa?

❶ Anorexia nervosa is a condition where the individual either refuses to eat an adequate amount of nourishing food or, by using laxatives or vomiting, doesn't allow ingested food time to be absorbed, resulting in emaciation. The condition occurs mainly in females (20:1), and the common age of onset is usually between 13 and 18 years, although it can occur later.

❷ The potential anorexic is typically introverted, sensitive and isolated, and tries to live up to the expectations of others. She (or he) becomes withdrawn, feels helpless and depressed. Family and cultural influences give her the idea that losing weight will alleviate her distress. Initial successful weight loss results in feelings of self-control and is positively encouraged by others. This is soon followed by a fear of weight gain.

❸ This self-destructive behaviour is often accompanied by a denial of concern over health. Patients may not recognise that they need help. Self-imposed starvation is a result of an overwhelming fear of increasing weight and losing control over appetite.

❹ Behind the eating behaviour, there are often numerous fears and anxieties. Often, with adolescent girls, there is a fear of growing up and assuming responsibility for themselves, or they may have a low opinion of themselves compared with others. For older women, there may be anxieties connected with pregnancy or dissatisfaction with their partner. Underlying most eating disorders is a low self-esteem and a tendency to link self worth to body weight and shape.

❺ Anorexia always arises in a social context, and so refusal to eat reflects a refusal to communicate deep, still unacceptable, feelings to others. In turn the parents' or partner's reaction is initially one of puzzlement which then changes to hurt, anger and hopelessness. A vicious circle quickly arises where each side's behaviour is making the situation worse.

Treatment of anorexia nervosa

❶ Treatment consists of two stages. The first priority is for the patient to gain weight. A target weight to work towards should be negotiated – 90 per cent of average for age, height, weight and sex is usual. Food intake needs to be monitored, regular meals need to be established, high-calorie supplement and energy-rich drinks need to be made part of the diet. Efforts to bully and cajole the patient into gaining weight are inappropriate. Patients are often admitted to hospital and involved in a behavioural regime initially involving bed rest where weight gain is linked to winning certain privileges, such as using the telephone or going for a walk. The patient is weighed each day at the same time.

❷ The second stage involves psychotherapy with the patient and sometimes with the family. The function of the patient's behaviour is an important issue to explore. Is the anorexia becoming a focus for the family's energy and holding together a shaky parental marriage? Is the patient's role being subtly reinforced by a partner who wants his wife to be dependent on him?

❸ Challenge the patient to reconsider the links between self-esteem and body weight. Rebuild self-esteem. Challenge 'perfectionism' and 'all or nothing' thinking.

❹ Treating anorexia is a long-term effort and requires patience and understanding from all involved.

Anorexia Nervosa

'Adversity reveals genius'

– Horace –

■ Introduction

Whatever the cause of pain, whether from an injury such as a broken leg, a disease such as arthritis, an infection such as shingles, or even if the cause of the pain has never been discovered, there are things that you can do that might help. Firstly it is important to understand that there is not a simple one-to-one direct relationship between tissue damage and pain. It is not simple a message like a telephone call from your body to your brain saying something is wrong. Rather, it is thought that nerve impulses from the tissue have to pass through a 'gate' situated in the spinal column and these impulses are altered by messages from the brain concerning how we think and feel. Some mental and emotional states open and some close this so-called 'pain gate'.

■ Factors which open the pain gate and pain gets worse

❶ **Physical damage:** The size and type of injury can influence the way we feel pain.

❷ **Low activity:** We notice pain much more if we are less active because activity has a distracting effect.

❸ **Depression/helplessness:** We can easily get into the vicious circle of doing less, which means we have fewer positive events in our lives and fewer opportunities for enjoyment. Our mood goes down and the pain becomes worse.

❹ **Anger:** If we are angry at the medical services for not providing a 'cure', or angry at the disability, asking 'why me?' our experience of pain is likely to increase.

❺ **Stress and tension:** Physical muscle tension opens the pain gate and we experience more pain.

❻ **Painwatching:** If you sit and think about your pain and notice it very carefully then it hurts more.

❼ **Fear about what the pain is:** Accurate information about the source of your pain is nearly always much less frightening than your secret worries about what is causing your pain. Many people secretly worry that there is something seriously wrong with them which can lead to an increase in tension.

❽ **Pain behaviour:** People only know about your pain by your pain behaviour, which includes things like grimacing, crying, moaning and complaining about the pain. Those around usually respond positively with sympathy and attention. It is easy to see how unconsciously tempting it must be to show a little more pain behaviour to remind others that all is not well. It is important for pain sufferers to look carefully at the messages they give out, as subconsciously the positive responses of others may be reinforcing or increasing the pain behaviour and your experience of pain.

❾ **Loss of independence:** If family and friends do things for the sufferer it is possible that the person will lose their independence. This engenders a loss of feelings of control which is likely to increase awareness of pain. Even if it takes two hours to prepare the vegetables and somebody else could have done them much quicker, it is still important to do the task to maintain that sense of independence and control.

■ Factors which close the pain gate and reduce the pain

❶ **Pain killers:** Some painkillers will make you notice the pain less.

❷ **Counter-stimulation:** Heat treatment, cold compresses or even massage can help spread the effects of the pain and close the pain gate.

❸ **Keeping busy:** Being busy helps switch your attention off the pain and helps close the pain gate.

❹ **Being relaxed:** Learning to relax and turn off tension reduces the pain messages getting through.

❺ **Setting realistic goals for your life:** Achieving small goals helps to reduce feelings of helplessness and tension.

 P

❶ Learn to relax and reduce your tension: When we are in pain it is common to tense up and hold our muscles very rigid, often in an unusual posture to try to protect the painful area. This is called 'muscle guarding'. Unfortunately, far from alleviating pain it usually makes it worse, because it causes tension and discomfort in other parts of the body. Learn a muscle relaxation exercise, and practice slow calm breathing. Identify ways that you relax generally such as having a hot bath, watching T.V, or listening to music.

❷ Keep a Pain diary: Be a detective and discover the pattern of your pain. Keep a diary and rate your pain on a scale of 1 to 10, identify the situations, and times when the pain increases or decreases. Adapt your daily programme so that the more important things are done when you hurt less.

❸ Challenge your negative thoughts: Write down your negative thoughts such as, 'I feel awful', 'I can't cope', and 'This pain is getting worse', then draw up a list of positive challenges such as, 'I am going to get on top of this', If 'I relax and distract myself it will improve'. Write down these challenging thoughts on the back of a postcard, and read them when you feel bad. Be aware of the tendency to 'catastrophise' and think in 'all or nothing ' terms.

❹ Distract yourself from the pain: As a rule if you focus on the pain it makes it worse. Distract yourself with interesting activity, enjoyable company, or an absorbing television programme. You will notice the pain less. Plan your day so that you have less time to focus on the pain.

❺ Use a visualisation technique: Some people can visualise their pain in a way that helps to control it. One man visualised the pain in his back as being, 'like a number of hot bars of an electric fire'. To control his pain he imagined switching each bar off, one by one, and visualised the glowing orange colour fading to a dull grey colour. Another technique involves building up a scene in your mind of a relaxing pain free situation such as a warm beach or a deep wood. If you can visualise yourself in that place using this form of guided imagery you can take yourself away from the pain.

❻ Pace yourself – avoid the all or nothing approach: Often people will either do too much or too little. If they feel well they might try to do all the things that they hadn't done when they felt bad, this might mean starting the day in a flurry of activity, then having to retreat to bed. This is not helpful. The ideas of pacing are: a) Take regular rests and enjoy breaks rather than waiting until you need them. b) Increase activity in a gradual stepwise progression – little and often.

❼ Set realistic goals: Look to the future and decide what you would like to achieve. Write down a number of specific goals for the short medium and long term. Then break these goals down into specific activities needed to achieve these goals. Set yourself targets for each day, even if this is something like walking the dog for 10 minutes or preparing the vegetables.

❽ Recognise the important effect of family and friends: Although it is difficult to advise those around you not to react to 'winces', 'moans', and other pain behaviour, as although it is an opportunity to show they care, it acts to reinforce the pain and make it worse. Ask them to try and ignore the pain behaviour and instead give praise and encouragement for effort and achievement. Ask them not to do things for you unless absolutely necessary as an overprotective carer can diminish your independence, which will ultimately mean that you have more time to focus on the pain.

Irritable Bowel Syndrome, often called IBS, is a malfunction in the way in which our digestive system works, or the way in which the food we eat moves through the intestine. The main symptoms include abdominal pain, and bouts of diarrhoea and constipation. The malfunction is closely related to how your intestine relates to stress and diet. IBS is surprisingly common: between 8 and 17 per cent of people in the developed world suffer from it.

People's reactions vary from healthy robust individuals who accept their symptoms and pay little attention, to others who fear moving to far away from a lavatory and have allowed their digestive system to become the focal point of their lives. People typically worry about being in situations where there is not immediate access to a toilet, which leads to anxiety which adversely affects the intestine and bowel. A vicious circle of worry leading to physical symptoms, leading to more worry and avoidance behaviour is created, very much like classical agoraphobia, but instead of worrying about having a panic attack the IBS sufferer worries about unexpected incontinence.

■ Managing IBS

❶ **Learn a relaxation technique:** A progressive muscle relaxation technique involving alternatively tensing and relaxing selected groups of muscles is helpful.

❷ **Progressively confront situations you have avoided:** If you start to avoid situations, such as going into new areas where you are not aware of the availability of a toilet, or driving on motorways, or going out in the morning without emptying your bowel, you are starting a slippery slope, where the more you avoid the worse your anxiety will become. Turn this process around and start to progressively confront those previously avoided situations. Draw up a hierarchy of difficult situations, rating each on a scale of 1 to 10 in terms of how anxious you feel. Then start at the easiest item and confront those situations, using anxiety management techniques such as, relaxation, distraction,

and positive self-talk. Watch your confidence return.

❸ **Challenge those 'catastrophic' thoughts:** People with IBS tend to 'catastrophise' in a number of areas. Firstly, they over-estimate how little control they will have over their symptoms. Secondly, they exaggerate how awful the mess would be if an unexpected incontinence occurred. Thirdly, they over-estimate how much people would notice. Fourthly, they over-estimate how negatively other people will view them. Challenge these distorted catastrophic thoughts, by looking at the evidence and the consequences of thinking that way. Alternatively, rather than challenging those thoughts themselves, use the 'downward arrow technique', and constantly ask yourself, 'What would be so bad about that?' This helps you to explore your worst possible fears and to accept that once you have accepted the reality it is often not as bad as the fantasy.

❹ **Eat regular healthy meals:** Never hurry your food, eat slowly. Make time for a leisurely breakfast. Eat high-fibre, low-fat foods such as wholemeal bread, fruit, vegetables, dried fruit, lentils and beans, and drink plenty of water.

❺ **Keep physically active:** Physical activity improves body functioning and takes your mind off symptoms. Exercises that strengthen abdominal muscles, such as sit-ups, are said to be helpful.

❻ **Manage your stress:** Your symptoms maybe a signal that you are under too much stress. Look to make changes if necessary.

◼ Introduction

There are no definitive tests for chronic fatigue but the primary symptoms are as follows:

a Fatigue is the principle symptom.
b It has a definite onset.
c It has been present for a minimum of six months and for more than 50 per cent of the time
d Other symptoms may be present such as muscle or joint pain, poor sleep, mood disturbances, headache, dizziness, sore throat, difficulty concentrating and memory problems.

It is a simplistic mistake to think in terms of either physical or mental causes of fatigue as both are closely intertwined. We know that there is a very close relationship between the brain and the immune system and the way a person thinks and behaves certainly seems to influence the effects of fatigue. A number of factors have been linked with causing fatigue which are as follows:

a Failure to get over viral illness (two-thirds of cases attribute fatigue to a viral trigger).
b Stress and busy lifestyle.
c Perfectionistic, achieving personality traits.

Fatigue syndrome is often characterised by the person either doing too much or doing too little physical activity. There seems to be a see-saw or yo-yo affect on activity levels where one day the person might do too much and the next day they would do too little. Doing less may help in the short term but in the long term inactivity makes you feel more exhausted and lethargic. Inactivity leads to loss of drive and determination, reduces your level of physical fitness and muscular strength, and effects the quality of your sleep. Patients who take to their beds lose 10 per cent of the power in their muscles in the first week.

◼ How to overcome chronic fatigue

❶ Gradually increase your activity levels. Set yourself a programme of gradually increasing activities starting with least difficult tasks and gradually, slowly, build up to more difficult tasks. Undertake activity for short periods of time – 'little and often' eg, 5 × 5 minutes a day rather than 25 minutes together. Balance activities that are enjoyable with activities that are not so enjoyable. Keep a diary or record sheet so that you can notice progress.

❷ Pace yourself. Avoid 'bursts' of activity followed by periods of exhaustion and rest.

❸ Follow a regular sleep pattern – 80 per cent of people with chronic fatigue have sleeping difficulties as they either sleep too much, or are not able to sleep through the night. Try to follow a regular sleep pattern, get up and go to bed at regular times and do not catnap during the day.

❹ Challenge distorted 'all or nothing', or 'catastrophic' thinking which may adversely effect your behaviour. For example you may say to yourself, 'I'm making myself ill', or 'I should try harder', or 'I'll be wiped out for a couple of weeks now'. Write down your negative thoughts on a diary sheet and challenge those thoughts.

❺ Distract yourself from becoming over sensitised to your bodily symptoms. Very often people become so aware of bodily symptoms of fatigue or muscle pain that this makes them worse. The more you think about a particular symptom the worse it is likely to get.

❻ Improve your diet. Eat a healthy balanced diet, three times a day, avoid drinking alcohol, and eliminate smoking as both increase level of fatigue.

❼ Expect setbacks and relapses as they are a normal part of progress – do not let them demoralise you.

'Health is harmony; disease is discord'

– Aristotle –

When we are stressed we subconsciously tense our shoulders, head and neck muscles. Nine out of ten headaches are tension headaches, or are due to contractions or stretching of muscles in the neck, shoulders and scalp – particularly the frontalis and temporalis muscles. These muscles must relax before pain can retreat. The other major type of headache is migraine headache, often occurring on one side of the head and sometimes associated with nausea and vomiting. Migraine headache is due to vasodilatation or swelling of blood vessels and tissues surrounding the brain. Vasodilatation and the pain that goes with it are thought to be caused by the release of the stress hormone serotonin. In reality there is often not a very clear distinction between these two types of headache. Both can be caused by a variety of triggers either emotional or physical.

Certain physical triggers which need to be excluded include: poor eyesight or a weakness in certain eye muscles, causing you to strain the other muscles to maintain normal binocular vision; sinus trouble or catarrh, which makes your head feel blocked up; menopause and menstruation; high blood pressure.

■ Ways of reducing headache

❶ **Keep a headache diary:** Record when and where your headache occurs. Look for a pattern and potential triggers.

❷ **Relaxation:** Progressive muscle relaxation training where muscle groups are first tensed and then relaxed has been shown to be effective especially if focused on the head, neck and shoulder muscles.

❸ **Massage and movement:** Massage the temples, squeezing gently at the base of the neck, resting your palms on closed eyes and pressing your finger tips on the side of your head above the eyes. Sometimes just moving around to music stretching the muscles in the neck and head can also help.

❹ **Hot and cold:** A warm bath, a hot water bottle on the neck, a warm towel on the head or face, or a cold flannel or cold compress can all help to relax muscles.

❺ **Diet:** Headache and migraine in particular can be caused by trigger foods such as chocolate, cheese, dairy products, alcohol (most noticeably red wine), caffeine (in coffee, tea and cola), fried food, citrus fruits and nuts.

❻ **Low blood sugar:** Headaches can also be linked to low blood sugar so beware of skipping meals. Always have breakfast. Do not replace meals with sugary snacks. Sometimes having a bite to eat can prevent a headache.

❼ **Relaxation:** Alter your stressful lifestyle and introduce more times of relaxation.

❽ **Retreat:** Some people find it helpful to lie down in a darkened room and relax or sleep.

❾ **Scents and salts:** Lavender oil, vapour rub, or other aromatic oil placed on finger tip and massaged gently into the temples, or placed on the pillow at night, can often lift away oppressive aches and tensions.

Antecedent Behaviour Consequence

DAY/TIME	ANTECEDENT What was happening? Where?	BEHAVIOUR What did you do?	CONSEQUENCE What happened then? How did you feel?

Self-Monitoring Sheet 2

Weekly Record

TIME/DAY	MONDAY	TUESDAY	WEDNESDAY	THURSDAY	FRIDAY	SATURDAY	SUNDAY
TOTAL							

P

'First you take a drink, then the drink takes a drink, then the drink takes you'

– F Scott Fitzgerald –

One standard unit of alcohol = One half-pint of average strength beer or lager, *or*
One glass of wine, *or*
One standard single measure of spirits.

Note: a can of high strength beer or lager may contain 3–4 units.

Recommendations for men
If your total for the week is more than 28 units you should consider cutting down.

Recommendations for women
If your total for the week is more than 21 units you should consider cutting down.

A heavy drinker
A heavy drinker is somebody who drinks more than the recommended units. If you are a heavy drinker, as compared to a light drinker you are:

◆ twice as likely to die of heart disease;

◆ twice as likely to die of cancer;

◆ twelve times more likely to die of cirrhosis of the liver;

◆ three times more likely to die in a road traffic accident;

◆ six times more likely to commit suicide.

If you have ever been physically dependent on alcohol for 6 months, or addicted, then any alcohol is likely to be harmful. You are likely to find it difficult to become a social or 'controlled' drinker and it is best to abstain altogether.

■ Other facts

◆ Approximately four times as many people in Britain are now experiencing serious problems related to their drinking than in the early 1960s.

◆ Cirrhosis of the liver is up by 60 per cent since 1955 in Britain.

◆ Alcohol dulls the action of the brain. Although it initially feels stimulating, it has a depressant effect.

◆ The body gets rid of alcohol by the liver oxidizing it. It takes the liver one hour to burn up a standard unit of alcohol.

◆ Hangovers are caused partly by impurities in alcoholic drinks, partly by dehydration and partly by low blood sugar. The darker in colour the drink, the more likely it is to cause a hangover.

◆ Alcohol is a diuretic, that is, it makes you urinate more than normal. Over a night's drinking, your body will lose more than it absorbs. For some people drinking a great deal of water before sleeping helps to avoid hangovers.

◆ Excessive drinking by pregnant women may harm the foetus. It is safest not to drink at all when you are pregnant.

◆ In the UK 50 per cent of all alcohol is drunk by 10 per cent of all drinkers.

❶ Make a decision to cut down and make a written contract with yourself to try your hardest to do so. Then tell others about that decision.

❷ Make three lists. First, list all the problems that you have that might be associated with drinking too much eg, poor health, problems at work, damaged relationships. Second make a list of all the reasons why you like drinking. You need to recognise these in order to be able to tackle changing your lifestyle. Third, list all your reasons for wanting to cut down eg, I want to be a better father.

❸ Keep a weekly drinking diary. Record times of drinking, how much you drank, where and who with. Total your consumption in units of alcohol for the week. (Remember one unit = one half-pint of beer, one glass of wine, or one measure of spirits.)

❹ Identify your most vulnerable high risk times of the day or week and who you are likely to be with. See if there is any pattern to your drinking. For example, mood states, feeling good or bad, rows or conflicts, or social situations.

❺ Work out a set of drinking rules for yourself and write them down.

Examples
I will never drink before 8pm.
I will never drink for more than three hours at a time.
I will stop drinking with Tony.
I will stop drinking strong lager.

❻ Keep at least two separate days of the week alcohol free and try to make these routine. This gives your body a chance to offset some of the impact of drinking.

❼ Have a daily cut-off point. Set yourself a rule that you will not drink more than, say, seven units of alcohol on any one day. It is important to recognise that once you have drunk over 3 or 4 units it becomes increasingly difficult to say 'no'.

❽ Slow down. Pace your drinking; if you are going to be in a pub for three hours and you only want to have three pints, then that is one every hour, perhaps interspersed with non-alcoholic drinks. Take smaller sips. Always put your glass down between sips. Occupy yourself (eg, play darts or dominoes).

❾ Reward your successes. If you achieve your goals, go out and buy yourself a special present.

❿ Look for alternatives to alcohol. This involves looking at why you drink. Is it to reduce anxiety or boredom, to increase confidence, or to beat feelings of depression? Do something else about these problems.

⓫ If you get a craving, delay your drinking for as long as possible. Distract yourself. Challenge your thoughts: 'I really need a drink', 'Rubbish, I don't *need* a drink. I want a drink because I feel tense'.

⓬ Expect occasional relapses and don't be devastated by them. Old habits are hard to break. A lapse does not have to mean a full relapse. Keep trying.

P

Drinking Diary

DAY	TIME FROM/TO	PLACE	WHO WITH	UNITS OF ALCOHOL	MONEY SPENT	CONSEQUENCES (IF ANY)

Why do You Drink?

I drink because I am bored	Rarely	Frequently
I drink because my friends drink	Rarely	Frequently
I drink because it helps me to relax	Rarely	Frequently
I drink because it makes me feel good	Rarely	Frequently
I drink to forget my problems	Rarely	Frequently
I drink because I like the taste	Rarely	Frequently
I drink because it gives me confidence	Rarely	Frequently
I drink in order to celebrate	Rarely	Frequently
I drink because it makes me feel at ease	Rarely	Frequently
I drink because I feel I have to	Rarely	Frequently
I drink to be sociable	Rarely	Frequently
I drink because there is nothing else to do	Rarely	Frequently
I drink to be polite	Rarely	Frequently
I drink when I feel under pressure	Rarely	Frequently
I drink when I feel angry	Rarely	Frequently
I drink when I feel really bad	Rarely	Frequently
I drink when I feel good	Rarely	Frequently
Try to think of any other reasons for your drinking and write them below:		
I drink		
I drink		
I drink		
I drink		
I drink		

 P

One standard unit of alcohol = One half-pint of average strength beer or lager, *or*
One glass of wine, *or*
One standard single measure of spirits.

Note: a can of high strength beer or lager may contain 3–4 units.

1 How often do you have a drink containing alcohol?
(0) Never
(1) Monthly or less
(2) 2–4 times a month
(3) 2–3 times a week
(4) 4 or more times a week

2 How many units of alcohol do you drink on a typical day when you are drinking?
(0) 1 or 2
(1) 3 or 4
(2) 5 or 6
(3) 7, 8 or 9
(4) 10 or more

3 How often do you have six or more units of alcohol on one occasion?
(0) Never
(1) Less than monthly
(2) Monthly
(3) Weekly
(4) Daily or almost daily

4 How often during the last year have you found that you were not able to stop drinking once you had started?
(0) Never
(1) Less than monthly
(2) Monthly
(3) Weekly
(4) Daily or almost daily

5 How often during the last year have you failed to do what was normally expected of you because of drinking?
(0) Never
(1) Less than monthly
(2) Monthly
(3) Weekly
(4) Daily or almost daily

6 How often during the last year have you needed a first drink in the morning to get yourself going after a heavy drinking session?
(0) Never
(1) Less than monthly
(2) Monthly
(3) Weekly
(4) Daily or almost daily

7 How often during the last year have you had a feeling of guilt or remorse after drinking?
(0) Never
(1) Less than monthly
(2) Monthly
(3) Weekly
(4) Daily or almost daily

8 How often during the last year have you been unable to remember what happened the night before because you had been drinking?
(0) Never
(1) Less than monthly
(2) Monthly
(3) Weekly
(4) Daily or almost daily

9 Have you or someone else been injured as a result of your drinking?
(0) No
(2) Yes but not in the last year
(4) Yes, during the last year

10 Has a relative or friend or doctor or another health worker been concerned about your drinking or suggested you cut down?
(0) No
(2) Yes but not in the last year
(4) Yes, during the last year

Record total of specific items here
If total over 8, alcohol use disorder very likely

This questionnaire was developed by the World Health Organisation to identify persons whose alcohol consumption has become hazardous or harmful to their health.

AUDIT (Alcohol Use Disorders Identification Test)

'Anger is the first emotion human beings experience and the last we learn to manage'

– Colleen Kelley –

■ Introduction

Anger is one of the first emotions we experience as very small babies. It is a natural emotion borne out of frustration and is a positive and constructive aid to survival. Its function is to provide us with a vital boost of physical and emotional energy just when we need it most. Anger can become a problem when it occurs too frequently, is too intense, lasts too long, when it leads to aggression, or when it disrupts our relationships. It has been said that anger wrecks more relationships than any other emotion. When our anger is creating problems for us either at work or at home we need to learn ways of controlling it.

Anger can be defined as an emotional state induced by an impulse to attack, defend or protect as a *response to a perceived threat or challenge.* That perceived threat or fear can be triggered by an insult, verbal abuse, physical assault, frustration, injustice, unfairness, criticism or annoyance. Anger is often the emotional reaction to very basic, childlike feelings of loss, hurt, abandonment or failing to get a basic need met.

When we get angry a subtle chain of observable events occurs. We may think that we just 'snap', but that is not the case. That chain includes

a an external trigger when something happens,
b our interpretation of that trigger which is the thought or mental statement we make to ourselves,
c our increased level of physical arousal (muscles tense, heartbeat increased, breathing becoming more rapid).

Often this chain of events occurs so quickly and automatically we are not aware of what has gone on. Anger management is about recognising, breaking down and altering this sequence of events.

■ Principles of anger management

❶ Aggression is a learnt behaviour which can be changed. Although we are all born with a potential to be aggressive we learn ways of channelling that impulse and behaving.

❷ Our core beliefs and our thoughts affect the way we behave. For example if we believed that 'life should always be fair', we would be continuously disappointed, frustrated and angry. The more 'shoulds', 'oughts' and high expectations we hold, the greater the tendency to get angry.

❸ If we can become more aware of and understand our thinking patterns and beliefs, and alter them, we can reduce our tendency to become angry.

❹ Anger has a physiological component. If we can become more aware of increasing levels of arousal such as increased heart rate and muscle tension we can use coping strategies to reduce this arousal, eg, relaxation.

❺ Identification of the triggers that make us feel angry helps us to anticipate and cope better as they arise.

❻ Loss of control is usually a result of a build up of small irritants that have not been dealt with. These may be external factors, such as financial worries, internal factors such as high expectations for ourselves, and interpersonal difficulties, such as relationship problems. Sometimes a final trigger, or 'last straw', can be something relatively minor.

❼ Anger is fuelled by an unbalanced, stressful, unhealthy lifestyle that does not have enough pleasures. We are more likely to get angry if we are already 'wound up'.

❽ Anger is often the result of poor problem solving, a limited repertoire of responses or difficulty in thinking of other ways of dealing with the situation.

❾ Anger can be a positive and empowering emotion if used constructively.

 P

❶ Carry out a cost-benefit analysis: List all the benefits (positive consequences) and costs (negative benefits) of losing your temper. Then imagine the benefits and costs of not getting angry.

❷ Express yourself assertively: Ventilating your feelings at the time reduces the tendency for anger and resentment to build up and eventually explode. Practise saying, 'I feel angry because . . .' and own your own anger.

❸ Anticipate the triggers: Keep a personal anger diary. Record the external triggers, your own thoughts, feelings and behaviour, and the effectiveness off various coping strategies. Then try and identify a pattern, count frequency and monitor change.

❹ Identify and express the feeling beneath the anger: (eg, hurt, fear, rejection, threat). For example, a father gets angry with his adolescent step-daughter for criticising him. The feeling of anger is covering up a feeling of hurt and rejection. How much better would it be for that man to say, 'It really hurts me when you say that'. Such a reaction has a much less negative consequence.

❺ Identify and challenge your rigid 'should' beliefs: Examine the core beliefs underlying your anger. It is not other people who make you angry, rather you make yourself angry because of a cluster of beliefs that you have in your head. Research suggests that there is over-use of the 'should' word. Common beliefs include; 'I *should,* must, or ought to be treated in a particular way', 'People *should* behave in a particular way', 'the world *should* be just and fair'. Alongside this, there are also beliefs that, 'who ever has done this to me *should* be chastised or punished in some way'. The more rigid these beliefs, the more likely that there will be frustration and a surge of anger. Identify and challenge some of these beliefs, soften them up, try to substitute 'it would be nice if' for 'should'. Alternatively, ask yourself 'why should this be so?'

❻ Prepare positive self-statements: This involves identifying key thoughts that you can write down and then repeat to yourself at times of high provocation. An example might be a parent trying to prevent himself from getting angry with his children. The three key self statements all begin with the letter 'C', which makes recall easier: 'they are just **children**, just playing', 'this is a real **challenge**, treat it as a challenge', 'stay **calm**, try to stay relaxed'. Other key self statements might include, 'don't take it personally', or, 'I don't need to prove myself'. If you can conjure up these thoughts in that split second before anger takes off, you may be able to stay in control.

❼ Learn to relax: Learn a muscle relaxation exercise.

❽ Manage your stress: Do not allow unfinished business to build up, look after your own needs, maintain a balance in your life.

❾ Develop a calming routine: If you notice yourself getting physically tense this should be your cue to go through the following routine.
  a Speech – speak slowly in a calm voice.
  b Distance – take a few steps backwards.
  c Relax your muscles – drop your shoulders, loosen your hands, relax your jaw.
  d Slow breathing – take 2 or 3 slow, deep breaths, from your stomach not your chest.
  e Distraction – count to ten or imagine a peaceful scene.
  f Humour – attempt to see the funny side of the situation.
  g Put yourself in the other person's shoes.

❿ Be Prepared: Prepare and rehearse how you will react in difficult situations

⓫ Leave the situation: If you feel you are 'losing it', remove yourself from the situation and allow yourself to calm down before returning.

Ways of Managing Anger

'Love cures people – both the ones who give and the ones who receive'

– Carl Menninger –

Exercises for Relationship Enhancement 1

❶ Identify similarities and differences: Accepting that our partners are different from ourselves is very important. Take a large piece of paper and on one half make a list of all the ways that you and your partner are alike, and on the other half make a list of all the ways you are different. This includes interests, attitudes, skills, likes, dislikes, personality and general outlook. Do the exercise separately and then get together and show each other your lists. Discuss the aspects in which you are alike and different. Go through the list of differences and identify differences that you are happy with and would like to continue, and those that you find hard to accept and would like the other person to change.

❷ Let's make a contract: Each partner draws up a list of the specific 'behaviours' that they would like their partner to increase, or do more of, and the specific behaviours they would like their partner to decrease or do less of. Then both partners agree to exchange a behaviour, of equal difficulty, and agree to make a contract. For example, 'I will put the top on the toothpaste everyday and you will put the toilet seat down'. It is best to start on small discrete tasks that are relatively easy to achieve and gradually work up to more difficult tasks.

❸ Rediscover spontaneity: After a while, couples get to know each other inside out, and routines become predictable. Make a deliberate effort to do things differently, breaking old familiar habits. For example sleep on the other side of the bed, dress differently, sit in a different chair to watch television, get up very early, tell a joke, miss a meal. Make a game out of guessing what the spontaneous thing was.

❹ Make a date: Coordinate your diaries and make a deliberate effort to spend some special time alone together each week. Perhaps having a leisurely meal together, or sitting and talking over a drink, or going out to see a show.

❺ Do you get the appreciation you deserve? Relationships can suffer when people do not feel appreciated, or when signs of appreciation, however small, are not forthcoming. These small signs of appreciation are often referred to as 'strokes'. For a relationship to flourish each person needs to give their partner appropriate 'strokes'. List all the things that you do, at home or at work, for which you think you deserve strokes. Then go through the list and place a '+' next to items where you feel you get sufficient stokes, a '−' next to the items where you feel you do not get sufficient strokes, and a '=' sign next to items where the balance is just about right. Both do this separately and then exchange and discuss lists.

❻ Do it for me: Make an agreement to take it in turns, to ask your partner to do something for you that you would like. It does not have to be anything spectacular, but rather something simple, and something that your partner would be able to do without feeling uncomfortable. Tasks might include watching a particular television programme together, cooking the evening meal, washing your hair for you, giving a massage, or going for a walk.

154

P

'Take away love and the earth is a tomb'
– Robert Browning

❼ The little things are important: Look at the following checklist of simple relationship enhancing tasks and tick off the ones that you do regularly.

1 Kiss or touch when saying goodbye or returning.	
2 Bring surprise presents; flowers, a card or chocolates.	
3 Ask about your partner's day. Discuss what happened.	
4 Plan a night out in advance.	
5 Compliment your partner on his or her appearance.	
6 Cuddle and be affectionate without sex.	
7 Touch hands when talking or walking.	
8 Make partner a cup of tea or drink.	
9 Ask your partner for advice.	
10 Look after your partner if he or she is unwell.	
11 Engage in joking and teasing.	
12 Do your fair share of work around the home.	
13 Discuss personal feelings and problems.	
14 Make time to do things together.	
15 Show anger in front of your partner.	
16 *Add your own.*	

❽ Write a structured letter: When we feel angry, disappointed or frustrated it is sometimes difficult to communicate in a loving way. Venting extreme emotion may create hurt and a vicious circle of retaliation. Writing your feelings down in a structured way releases some of the intensity, allows you to explore more than one feeling, moves you on to feelings of love, and assists you in telling the whole truth and not just part of it. This exercise involves writing a letter to your partner expressing your feelings in five sections. Start with 'I feel angry that . . .', 'I feel sad that . . .', 'I feel afraid that . . .', 'I regret that . . .' and 'I love . . .' Write a few sentences about each feeling. Complete all sections – do not stop until you get to love.

❾ Open talk: Set aside a period when each partner has the opportunity to talk openly and the other has to listen without comment or interruption. Agree on a set time period between 5 and 20 minutes. Then decide who is going to go first. Then the first person says what is on their mind and how they are feeling. Then change roles. Make an agreement that either partner can ask for an open talk at any time.

'There is no norm in sex. Norm is the name of the guy who lives in Brooklyn'

– Dr Alex Comfort –

⑩ Improving your sexual relationship: There is no such thing as a normal sexual relationship, rather we can talk in terms of a satisfactory sexual relationship, where both partners feel mutually satisfied. To have and maintain a fulfilling sexual relationship can help cement relationships together, reflect intimacy and ultimately relieve stress.

a *Communicate.* Talk about your love making, explain what you like and do not like, and your different needs. Talk while making love, saying, 'That's nice, I like you doing that'. Take active responsibility for your own pleasure by showing your partner what you like. Experiment, try out different things.

b *Be flexible.* A fulfilling sex life means recognising the need for flexibility and changeability. Your needs will be different on different occasions. Just as our appetite for food varies so does our appetite for sex. Occasionally we might want an elaborate three course meal, which involves planning and preparation, while at other times we might want a quick snack or a sandwich on the run. Similarly, our sexual appetite varies. This variety maintains interest. Imagine how boring a steady diet of the same encounter would be?

c *What turns you on.* With your partner take it in turns to describe what you like or find arousing about the following list. Do not interrupt but allow each to have their say. Looks, clothes, touching, kissing, stroking, manners, atmosphere, particular sexual words, sexual acts, foreplay, after sex.

d *Focus on the sensation.* Spend time just touching and stroking each other – use a massage oil. Resist the temptation to have full intercourse or reach a climax or even to touch each others' genitals.

e *Make time and make it special.* Deliberately make time for love making rather than always coming together when feeling tired at the end of the day. If things have become a little routine create a special atmosphere with soft lights, candles, music, or maybe after a bath. Make love somewhere other than in bed.

f *Overcome inhibition.* If you feel inhibited and have deeply ingrained beliefs that sex is 'dirty', 'sinful' or 'should not be discussed', try to re-examine your attitudes. Develop your fantasies by looking at erotic books, magazines or videos. Your imagination is a safe place to let your inhibitions go and to experiment with different feelings. Read a book of sexual fantasies. Practice losing control during love-making: breathe more heavily or moan more loudly.

P

> ‘Everything that irritates us about others can
> lead us on to an understanding of ourselves’
>
> – Carl Jung –

Consider which of the following unrealistic beliefs you hold:

1 **‘A relationship that needs to be worked on is not worth having’.**
All satisfying relationships require two committed people making an effort. Often the more difficult times you successfully come through the stronger the relationship. Good relationships simply do not just happen.

2 **‘The excitement and romance in our love will continue unabated over time’.**
Relationships change and go through phases as time passes. The early ‘fizz’ is usually gradually replaced by a mature, deeper understanding love.

3 **‘Being in an intimate relationship should be the way to happiness’.**
Your relationship is only one part of your life so do not expect it to make everything in your life magically alright.

4 **‘It’s the other person’s fault. If only they could change and be different’.**
Improving relationships is about changing yourself and not directly expecting the other person to change. The changes you make in yourself will precipitate changes in others. A good relationship is often not about choosing the right person, but being the right person.

5 **‘If my partner really loved me he or she would react and behave in a certain way – the way I behave’.**
Our partners are different from us and that is a good thing. When we can accept and respect our differences our relationship has a chance of blossoming.

6 **‘My partner should always know how I feel and should anticipate my needs’.**
Do not suppose that your partner telepathically knows how you feel. The ability to communicate honestly how you feel, and what you think, is the essential ingredient in a healthy relationship.

7 **‘My partner should provide everything I need. I do not need anybody else. Love means wanting to be together’.**
No one person can meet all our needs. We all need to maintain a healthy circle of friendships to meet our varied needs.

8 **‘My partner should never hurt me or strike back in anger or disagree with me on important matters’.**
You and your partner are different and, inevitably from time to time, will frustrate each other. We can all say things in anger that we do not mean. Tolerance and forgiveness are important ingredients.

■ Stage 1: Non-Genital Sensate Focus

This exercise is an opportunity for you to make a fresh start in your love life. The idea is to learn to enjoy giving pleasure to your partner by non-sexual contact through the experience of touch.

No sexual intercourse should take place during this stage, and there should be no touching of breasts, nipples, penis, testicles, vagina or clitoris. But you can kiss and cuddle as much as you like!

Make a specific time when you will both be relaxed and not rushed. Choose a place which is warm and comfortable. If the bedroom is cold, try sitting in front of the sitting room fire. Sometimes a warm bath beforehand can be relaxing.

Both partners should remove all items of clothing. One partner should approach the other partner who should be lying comfortably. Use a lotion to massage, fondle, and trace the outline of your partner's body. Try to discover the degree of pressure which is most enjoyable, and which areas of the body are most sensitive. The non-active partner is allowed to do nothing except concentrate on the thoughts and feelings aroused, and to give feedback on how, where, and in what way they enjoy being touched.

Now place your hand under your partner's hand so that you can guide it to areas that are pleasurable. Try one partner lying on their front, while the other massages their back, neck, shoulders, arms, buttocks and legs for 10 minutes, using the lotion to rub gently into the skin. Then change over. Next partner A can lie on their back while partner B massages neck, chest, stomach, shoulders, arms and legs.

Use your own imaginative variations and try the same exercise on three to four different occasions. Try to be relaxed and make the session into as much fun as possible.

■ Stage 2: Genital Sensate Focus

When both partners enjoy Stage 1 – non-genital sensate focus – and feel completely relaxed, you can begin to include genital areas into the session. Again the aim is to explore different ways of giving pleasure, with no specific goal of trying to achieve orgasm.

To start with, carry out the instructions for non-genital sensate focus. This time, each spend 10 minutes touching and massaging the other's body. Now partner A gently massages partner's B breasts and nipples for five minutes. Then partner B massages A's breasts and nipples for five minutes. Again the emphasis is on feedback and guidance – tell your partner what feels good.

The next steps are as follows: the man gently touches the woman's clitoris. The woman gently touches the man's testicles and penis. Each step should last five minutes.

The next step is best carried out with the man sitting up or leaning against a pillow with the woman sitting between his legs. She should then be stimulated according to her wishes using hand guidance if necessary. Stimulate the outer vagina and clitoris gently at first, then increase the speed of stimulation. Take a rest for a few minutes and then try again.

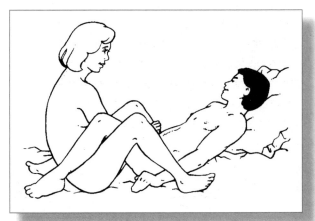

Change over to a position where the man is lying on his back. He can then show his partner how to rub his penis, testicles and thighs to produce an erection. Use moisturising lotion when

P

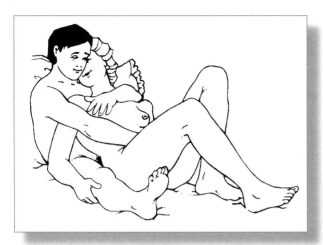

necessary. If either partner gets excited, they can be given a manual climax, but again this is not the aim of the exercise.

■ Stage 3: Intercourse

❶ When Stage 1 (non-genital sensate focus) and Stage 2 (genital state focus) have been completed, with both partners feeling fully relaxed and the man obtaining a full erection, you are ready for Stage 3.

❷ Go through Stage 1 briefly (10 minutes) and then Stage 2 (20 minutes). The next stage is to insert the penis into the vagina. It is best if the woman is in control of this at first. Adopt the female superior position, when the woman sits astride her partner with her knees at around the level of his chest. This position is important in all forms of sexual difficulty as it gets away from the traditional 'man on top' ideas, which some women find threatening, and gives the woman more control. It allows a man with potency or ejaculatory problems to relax more.

❸ With the woman kneeling astride the man, stroke and caress his penis. Take your time, there is no rush. When you are both excited, rub his penis against your clitoris and vagina. When you feel pleasure, tell him. As he becomes excited, guide his penis into your vagina. It is not necessary for the penis to be fully erect at this stage. Keep still. Pause and relax, enjoying the feeling of contact between penis and vagina. Only as you become more familiar with the position, move around gently backwards and forwards on the penis. Remember you need not be afraid of too deep penetration as this can be controlled by your leaning forward.

❹ Ask your partner to move more when you both feel ready for it. If either if you requires more manual stimulation of clitoris or penis, you can do this. Remember to keep communicating and giving each other feedback.

❶ Overcoming the problem of premature ejaculation can be viewed as the man learning to perceive and control the sensations prior to ejaculation. In some ways this is a little like a child learning to become continent by paying full attention to the sensations of a full bladder. The aim of the following techniques is to make the man more aware of those sensations, and to develop greater control by raising his threshold of excitation and subsequently ejaculation.

❷ Two techniques have been proposed that are very similar in their thinking: the 'pause' or 'stop-start' technique, and the 'squeeze' technique. Both involve creating an erection and a high level of arousal, then interrupting it prior to ejaculation. With the interruption or withdrawal of stimulation, arousal levels plateau and then subside. Stimulation can then be continued after a break of 20 to 30 seconds.

a The 'squeeze technique', put forward by Masters and Johnson in 1970, involves the female partner stimulating the penis manually until her partner indicates that he is nearing ejaculation. The female then squeezes her partner's penis under and behind the glans around the coronal ridge. The pressure is applied for around three seconds. The squeeze should stop the urge to ejaculate. Then after 15 to 30 seconds, stimulation of the penis can start again, and then once again, prior to ejaculation, the penis can be squeezed.

b The 'pause' or 'stop-start' technique again involves stimulating the penis to the point prior to ejaculation. Stimulation is then stopped for 15 to 20 seconds. The man then learns to control the feelings and sensations. It is sometimes helpful deliberately to think non erotic and distracting thoughts which can break the cycle of arousal. To further increase control, initial stimulation should be carried out without lubrication, then once control is established, move on to using lubrication simulating vaginal conditions.

❸ The next stage after manual stimulation is to insert the penis into the vagina. The female superior position is best to start off with, as this offers the man the best chance of ejaculatory control. Initially, stay still and just experience the sensation, then start slow thrusts, but slow down or stop whenever you notice the sensations prior to ejaculation occurring.

❹ Sensitivity to reach orgasm very quickly can sometimes be reduced by using a condom, alcohol, renewing sexual activity one to two hours after having previously ejaculated, deliberately thinking non-erotic thoughts or increasing the frequency of intercourse. The more often you have reach orgasm in a given time period the lower will be your level of excitability.

P

Vaginisimus (painful intercourse)

This is a condition where intercourse is actually painful and the women finds herself squeezing her pelvic muscles, or the muscles around the vagina, into spasm.

◆ Sensate focus concentrating on non-genital and genital areas is a good place to start, but remember full sexual intercourse is not the purpose of the exercise. Look at your own genitalia in a hand mirror and try to locate the sensitive parts by touching.

◆ Start experimenting by first putting the top of your little finger inside your own vagina and, as you get used to this, your whole finger and then two fingers. When you can accommodate two of your own fingers comfortably, allow your partner to insert a finger into your vagina slowly and gently until you are used to it.

◆ An alternative is to insert a small dilator into your vagina. These dilators are available in varying sizes and so it is a good idea to work up gradually to large dilators and to keeping them in for longer periods of time. As you feel more comfortable, the spasms will lessen and you can move on to a slightly larger size. Use the dilation procedure, then remove it and insert your partner's penis at your own pace.

◆ Graded vaginal dilators can be obtained from John Bell and Croydon, Wigmore Street, London W1.

Orgasmic dysfunction

◆ This is often initially a question of overcoming cultural brainwashing which conditions women to be the passive partner. Ignore all the nonsense which says that women do not initiate sex or get pleasure. Learn to move more vigorously during intercourse to stimulate yourself and teach your partner to move in ways which satisfy you.

◆ Try out both non-genital sensate focus and genital sensate focus, encouraging your partner to do what is pleasing to you. Remember that in both cases full sexual intercourse is banned; the exercise is about bringing your partner pleasure and being relaxed.

◆ Masturbation training programme. Look at your vagina in a small hand mirror. Stimulate yourself. Try making circular or up-and-down movements of your finger on your clitoris. Vary the speed of movement and pressure. If you are not moist enough try saliva or a baby lotion on your fingertips. Now try to imagine a sexual fantasy that you like while continuing to stimulate yourself. If you do not climax you can obtain a hand-held vibrator. Acquire books or a magazine which contain suitable sexual fantasies (Nancy Friday's *My Secret Garden,* Quartet, London, 1973 is highly recommended). Allow yourself the option of creating your fantasy.

	AGREE	DISAGREE
1 We both have common interests and like similar things.	1	0
2 I enjoy talking with my partner.	1	0
3 I can have fun and laugh with my partner.	1	0
4 My partner generally makes me feel loved and wanted.	1	0
5 My partner talks to me about how he/she is feeling.	1	0
6 My partner is usually sensitive and aware of my needs.	1	0
7 I trust my partner.	1	0
8 Our relationship is continually developing and evolving.	1	0
9 My partner respects me and what I do.	1	0
10 After a disagreement we can 'agree to disagree'.	1	0
11 We do have a fulfilling sexual relationship.	1	0
12 I can express both positive feelings, (eg, love) and negative feelings (eg, anger) to my partner.	1	0
13 I show affection to my partner.	1	0
14 When conflicts arise they are usually resolved quite quickly.	1	0
15 I am happy with our relationship.	1	0
16 I am totally committed to this relationship.	1	0
17 I accept my partner, and do not expect them to change.	1	0
18 It always helps to sit down and talk things through.	1	0
19 I think I am aware of my partner's 'needs' and 'likes'.	1	0
20 I feel emotionally close to my partner.	1	0

Scoring

Above 15 Good relationship
8–15 Average relationship – could be improved.
Below 8 Poor relationship – needs to be worked on.

P

SECTION 6 – CARING FOR OTHERS

CARING FOR OTHERS

Books for Professionals

Atkinson JM, *Schizophrenia at Home – A Guide to Helping the Family,* Croom Helm, London, 1986.

Falloon I, *Family Management of Schizophrenia*, John Hopkins University Press, Baltimore, Maryland, 1985.

Fussey I & Muir-Giles G, *Rehabilitation of the Severely Brain Injured Adult*, Croom Helm, London, 1988.

Holden UP, *Looking at Confusion – A Handbook for Those Working with the Elderly*, Winslow Press, Bicester, 1987.

Holden UP & Woods R, *Positive Approaches to Dementia Care*, Churchill Livingstone, Edinburgh, 2000.

Morton I, *Person-Centred Approaches to Dementia Care*, Winslow Press, Bicester, 1999.

Papadopoulous A, *Counselling Carers*, Winslow Press, Bicester, 1989.

Pillling S, *Rehabilitation and Community Care*, Routledge, London, 1991.

Stokes G, *Managing Common Problems with the Elderly Confused (Aggression; Incontinence and Inappropriate Urination; Screaming and Shouting; Wandering)*, Four books published by Winslow Press, Bicester, 1987.

Stokes G, *Challenging Behaviour in Dementia*, Winslow Press, Bicester, 2000.

Stokes G & Goudie F, *Working with Dementia*, Winslow Press, Bicester, 1990.

Twining C, *The Memory Handbook*, Winslow Press, Bicester, 1991.

Books for Clients

Woods B & Lay C, *Caring for the Person with Dementia – A Guide for Families and Other Carers,* Alzheimer's Disease Society, London, 1984.

Addresses

Age Concern, Astral House, 1268 London Road, London SW16 4ER.
Tel 020 8765 7200 and 0808 808 6060

Alzheimer's Disease Society, Gordon House, 10 Greencoat Place, London SW1P 9PH
Tel: 020 7306 0606 and 020 7300 0336 (helpline)

Association of Crossroads Care Attendants Scheme, Waymead, St Anthony's Close, Binfield Road, Bracknell, Berks RG42 2EB
Tel 01344 860677

Headway – National Head Injuries Association, 4 King Edward Court, King Edward Street, Nottingham NG1 1EW
Tel 0115 924 0800

Mental Health Act Commission, Maid Marian House, 56 Houndsgate, Nottingham NG1 6BG
Tel 0115 943 7100

MIND (National Association for Mental Health), Granter House, 15–19 Broadway, London E15 4BQ
Tel 020 8522 1728 and 08457 660163 (infoline)

National Association of Citizens Advice Bureaux, 115–123 Pentonville Road, London N1 9LZ
Tel 020 7833 2181

National Schizophrenia Fellowship, 27 Revel Close, Basingstoke, Hants RG22 4ED
Tel 01256 463834

SANE (Schizophrenia A National Emergency), 1st Floor, Cityside House, 40 Alder Street, London E1 1EE.
Tel 0345 678000 (helpline) and 020 7375 1002

Incidence

Schizophrenia is a major mental illness that can affect anybody. One person out of every hundred will probably suffer from schizophrenia before they reach the age of 45. In Britain, about 35,000 people are admitted to hospital every year with the illness. This makes up about one-sixth of all the people in hospital. Schizophrenia occurs all over the world.

The illness tends to strike people first between the ages of 18 and 35, very often when they are in their prime, and when they are trying to establish independent lives. It occurs in both men and women although it tends to start a little later in women.

Schizophrenia affects all aspects of the sufferers' lives, including the way they think, how they feel and the way they behave. Those affected may hear voices, develop strange delusional ideas, or become apathetic, lose interest and change emotionally. One of the difficulties is that those affected may themselves be unaware that something is wrong. For the sufferer it is difficult to decide what is real and what is not real. It is a little like having a dream while being wide awake.

Myths about schizophrenia

A number of popular misconceptions exist. The first is that schizophrenia is about having a multiple personality, like Dr Jekyll and Mr Hyde. This is completely untrue. Schizophrenia has nothing to do with being more than one personality; rather it can be regarded as a disintegration of personality. A second popular myth is that people who have schizophrenia are always dangerous and violent. Again this is untrue, as people with schizophrenia are often very timid and frightened and no more likely to commit violent crime than anybody else. A third myth is that schizophrenia is somehow the result of bad parenting. There is no scientific basis for this notion; an overwhelming amount of scientific evidence suggests that schizophrenia is a disease of the brain.

Diagnosis and outcome

Schizophrenia is a very difficult illness to diagnose and it is even more difficult to predict the outcome. There is no laboratory test for schizophrenia and the diagnosis is based on the patient's symptoms. About one-third of those affected have a single attack and recover completely. However, for others there may be further attacks or even an uninterrupted continuation of the symptoms. At the beginning of the illness it is not possible to tell who will recover and who will have to cope with long-term problems; that is why doctors and health workers are often slow or unwilling to reach a definite diagnosis and make firm predictions.

What is Schizophrenia?

Schizophrenia is difficult to recognise: there are no special tests for the illness and no outward physical signs. Very often people with schizophrenia don't want to talk about it. Sometimes symptoms are very slow to show up and no two people have the same array of symptoms.

There are two main types of symptoms which affect a person's thoughts, feelings and behaviour. First 'positive symptoms', which means something is added to the person's usual behaviour, for example, hearing voices or having delusional ideas. These positive symptoms normally occur during an acute attack and are often responsive to medication. Second 'negative symptoms', which means something is lost from the person, for example, this might include loss of energy, or interest, or being unable to demonstrate affection, or lacking appropriate feelings or reactions.

■ Positive symptoms

Hearing voices: also known as auditory hallucinations. Sufferers hear other people's voices in their head making comments about them or what they are doing. These voices can be experienced as both pleasant and unpleasant depending on what they say. The individual often responds to them as if they were real or have power over them.

Delusions: a highly improbable idea becomes fixed in the person's mind as a certainty and ordinary attempts to point out contradictions cannot shift it. Examples of these ideas might be that they have special powers (being God or the Prime Minister) or that somebody is trying to harm them.

Thought control: the person believes their mind is being controlled from outside, for example, by a radio receiver or aliens.

Thought broadcast: the person imagines their thoughts are being spoken out loud.

Thought disorder: ideas become loosely associated, disconnected and flighty. One idea leads very quickly to the next and it is difficult to concentrate or stay focused on one particular subject. Concentration becomes difficult.

Incoherent talking: speech becomes rather mixed up and rambling.

■ Negative symptoms

Loss of energy and motivation: the person may have no enthusiasm, activity levels are reduced and self-care is often neglected, the person may not want to get out of bed in the morning.

Withdrawal: the person may avoid social activities and external events, becoming more occupied with internal events or the thoughts and voices in their heads.

Emotional changes: emotions are not expressed normally; the person may appear emotionally flat or behave inappropriately, laughing at serious subjects.

Poverty of speech: initiation and content of speech is reduced, the person becomes quieter and has less need to communicate with the external world.

P

There are many different theories, but the fact remains that at present the causes of schizophrenia are not really known. There seems to be no single cause; rather, the consensus view is that certain people have an in-built predisposition or vulnerability which can be triggered at certain times, by certain events.

There is no evidence that families cause schizophrenia. A great deal of material was published in the 1960s and early 1970s linking schizophrenia to family life, but none of it was based on formal research. The result of these publications was that some families felt guilty, believing that they had brought the problem on in some way. A family is usually the most valuable help and support available to somebody with schizophrenia.

◼ Predisposing factors

Genetic: Research has shown that vulnerability to schizophrenia is affected by genetic factors. The average chance of developing schizophrenia is about 1 in 100. However, if one parent has schizophrenia, the chances that the child will develop it as an adult rise to 1 in 10. If both parents have it, the risk rises to a 4 in 10 chance. If an identical twin has the illness the risk to the other twin is nearly 1 in 2. However, over 60% of people with schizophrenia have no close family history with the disorder.

Brain chemicals and structure: Research has shown that schizophrenia is accompanied by subtle changes in the chemicals in the brain. These chemical are called neurotransmitters and they allow nerve cells in the brain to do their jobs. A popular idea is that there is too much of one chemical called dopamine. Some forms of medication appear to correct that chemical imbalance. It is now well established that abnormalities in the brain are present in a large number of people with schizophrenia. Their brains are often 5 per cent smaller with slightly larger ventricles (the fluid-filled spaces in the middle of the brain).

Other studies: Other research has suggested problems may start at a very early stage of the brains development in the embryo or foetus, or be associated with birth difficulties.

◼ Trigger factors

Stress: appears to be a factor in setting off an attack if somebody has a predisposition to schizophrenia. Stress can include adverse life events such as losing a job, a bereavement, loss of a relationship, or moving away from home.

High expressed emotion: There is firm evidence that living in an environment where there is a great deal of expressed emotion is damaging to the schizophrenic's mental health. High expressed emotion means critical comments, hostility and emotional over-involvement with over-protectiveness and high expectations of close contact. Families and carers should be aiming for low expressed emotion, which means acceptance of the illness, tolerance and low-level intrusiveness, allowing the patient ample personal space.

Drug and alcohol abuse: Some drugs, especially stimulants, such as amphetamine and cocaine, or hallucinogenics, can trigger episodes.

Hormonal upheavals: Often in women after puberty, childbirth, or less frequently menopause.

There is no single cure for schizophrenia. Treatment ideally should consist of a number of components, such as medication, education of family, social and psychological treatment.

■ Medication

Acute schizophrenic symptoms can usually be brought under control by medication known variously as antipsychotics, neuroleptics, or major tranquillisers. These drugs can be taken either as tablets, or syrup, or in injection form. Injections are often more convenient and easier to remember than tablets. Major types of antipsychotic medication include Largactil, Modecate, Depixol and Piportil. These types of medication are often very effective in treating positive symptoms such as hallucinations and delusions, but less effective with negative symptoms (see p166). These medications often take a couple of weeks to reach full effect and, although relatives may see benefits, the actual sufferer may be less aware of them. Medication produces side-effects such as dry mouth, restlessness and tremor which can be controlled by other tablets like Procyclidine and Disipal. There are some new drugs known as 'atypical antipsychotics', such as Chorazil and Olanzapine, which have fewer side effects and are thought to help reduce negative as well as positive symptoms.

If a person with schizophrenia is taking medication, the risk of having a second attack within a year is reduced from approximately 75 per cent to 30 per cent. Medication not only helps recovery but has a preventative action.

■ Social & psychological treatment

Education: It is essential that any drug therapy goes hand-in-hand with education of the patient and family. Each patient needs the right balance of understanding, social stimulation and privacy.

Social therapy and structure: Social therapy carried out in drop-in centres or mental health centres is particularly good for people with negative symptoms such as lack of energy and motivation. Having a structured daily timetable is vitally important for those who find it so difficult to structure their days and might otherwise stay in their room all day and not look after themselves.

Psychological therapy: Individual counselling is often helpful and gives the sufferers an opportunity to talk about problems of everyday living, and to feel less isolated and more in control of their lives. Gaining insight and understanding of the illness can certainly help.

Self-monitoring and learning coping strategies: Teaching people to self-monitor their own symptoms, so that they can recognise early on when they are worsening, can help reduce the number of relapses. Developing coping strategies (distraction, relaxation etc) for dealing with symptoms also helps the suffer to feel more in control and better able to cope.

 P

A young woman's description of thinking and over-arousal:

'My thoughts get all jumbled up. I start thinking about something but never quite get there. My trouble is that I've got too many thoughts constantly coming into my head. Sometimes I'll try and think about something like my car and a dozen different thoughts about my car would come into my head at the same time. I open my mouth and people say I just talk a load of rubbish.'

A description from a young man of the onset of an acute episode of schizophrenia with prominent delusional ideas (positive symptoms):

'I was living on my own at the time – working in a bank. I'd worked out a new master plan for a complete system of living which I'd written down in lots of special notebooks. It was based on very complicated scientific equations and messages transmitted from car number plates. I kept thinking the communists were after me and the British Secret Service were protecting me. I ran away with a copy of the Bible in my pocket but was soon picked up by the police. I told them I'd murdered my brother so they put me in jail to protect me from the communists. Some time later a doctor and a social worker took me to hospital. I didn't resist because it was all part of the plan.'

This young man describes some of the negative symptoms he experienced after his first attack of schizophrenia:

'I used to love going out to clubs and dancing. I'd buy all the records. I loved playing football and watching it on TV. But now I don't. I don't care anymore – I just can't see the point. I've got a son who's four years old – of course I love him, but I don't feel it here in my inside anymore. Every day is the same. A friend told me a joke the other day but I didn't laugh. It was funny but not funny enough. I can't be bothered to wash or brush my hair or even get up sometimes. I sleep all right most nights but sometimes I wake up in a sweat. I don't really see that there's much difference between being asleep and awake.'

■ Advice for carers of people with schizophrenia

People with schizophrenia do not like high levels of expressed emotion – critical remarks, arguments, conflicts, tears and excessive emotion.

The most important thing is to understand how a vicious circle can easily be established, involving emotional stress which exacerbates symptoms, creating more stress, and so on. Stress levels can be reduced by carers looking at their own behaviour and trying to reduce the general level of expressed emotion.

◆ **Understand and accept the illness for what it is.** Try not to blame the sufferer, and accept that he or she is not responsible for the present behaviour and circumstances. Watch out for thoughts like, 'She could stop it if she really wanted to'. Try to accept that the sufferer may not be able to express their love or gratitude in return.

◆ **Avoid global critical comments** such as, 'He's always been a lazy so-and-so'. Instead try to make clear specific statements using the word 'I'. For example, 'I would like you to make your bed', rather than, 'He never does anything in the house'.

◆ **Practise good listening skills.** Schizophrenia often affects the individual's speed of thought and speech. Allow the sufferer more time to talk and more time to respond.

◆ **Reduce personal intrusiveness** or repeated attempts to establish emotion contact. The illness of schizophrenia means that very often the sufferer wants a more limited degree of contact. It's difficult to accept, but their needs may have changed. Sometimes it is useful to deliberately reduce the amount of time in face-to-face contact. Give them space and time alone if they need it.

◆ **Beware of over-protectiveness** and over-involvement. Sufferers can easily feel trapped and guilty if they feel that carers have become extremely self-sacrificing. Leave them alone in the house for a while and go out and enjoy yourself. This may involve taking risks but it is extremely important. Remember the sufferer is an adult – do not treat them like a child.

◆ **Set limits and make contracts.** Talk about what the family considers to be acceptable and unacceptable behaviour. Make either formal written agreements or verbal agreements about negotiated changes in family members' behaviour. For example, the sufferer may agree to get up by a certain time in return for breakfast of his or her choice.

◆ **Take time out.** Both family members and the patient should be allowed to say when they feel a situation is getting more than they can deal with, and request time away from the situation. For example, the patient may say, 'I can only spend 30 minutes with the visitors, then I want to be on my own', or the family member might say, 'I can only listen to your problems for a certain length of time'. Find out about respite care.

◆ **Encourage some activity and socialising everyday.** A delicate balance is needed between overstimulation and understimulation.

◆ **Encourage the person to take their medication.** Schizophrenia is an illness, involving a chemical imbalance in the brain, and does respond to medication.

 P

Advice for people with schizophrenia

Often people with schizophrenia develop their own ways of coping with symptoms, such as playing music through headphones when hearing voices. The use of these 'coping strategies' does not necessarily remove the symptoms, but it often enables the person to feel more in control of those symptoms. Outlined here are some coping strategies that some people have found useful.

Self monitoring

An important first step in managing your own symptoms is to become more aware of them and how they affect you. Monitoring your own mood, symptoms and behaviour, by completing a short questionnaire every fortnight has been shown to be useful (Early Signs Scale pp172–73). The questionnaire includes early warning signs that you may be getting unwell. If symptoms are getting worse then positive steps can be taken, such as seeking further support, or preparing for a relapse. It can help to have another person's view, so why not ask a close friend or relative to fill in the questionnaire too.

Coping with positive symptoms

◆ **Distraction.** Distract attention from voices by keeping busy, talking to others, listening to a radio, using a personal stereo with ear plugs or with headphones or reading the newspaper.

◆ **Relaxation.** Practice relaxation exercises to relieve tension and anxiety. If you can relax yourself physically there is a good chance that your mind will relax.

◆ **Challenge the voices.** Seek help to understand and perhaps challenge what the voices say or challenge your worrying thoughts or delusional beliefs. Ask yourself 'What is the evidence for that particular thought?', 'How would someone else view this situation?' Prepare a number of positive thoughts such as, 'these voices are part of my illness and what they say is usually nonsense'. Write these thoughts on a card, and remind yourself of them when you hear the voices. Maybe whisper to yourself the positive challenging thoughts.

◆ **Find a creative outlet.** Have you tried painting or drawing, playing a musical instrument, writing poetry or short stories, woodwork or metal work?

◆ **Reduce your stress.** Try to maintain a balanced lifestyle. Avoid situations of high expressed emotion or people that 'wind you up'.

◆ **Take your medication regularly.**

Coping with negative symptoms

◆ **Build in structure and purpose to each day.** Perhaps keep a calendar or diary and plan activities, or make a 'to do' list on a sheet of paper or sticky label. Plan to go to support and activity groups.

◆ **Encourage social support.** Ask others to help you get going and provide support.

◆ **Keep active.** Have a range of interests and hobbies, including physical exercises.

◆ **Be positive.** Make a list of your achievements and feel positive about yourself.

Identify triggers

Most people can identify specific events or a series of events that make symptoms worse. These might include a sudden unexpected change in circumstances; having too much to do or excessive stimulation. Other triggers might be situations where there are people who are critical, hostile, over-protective or display excessive levels of emotion that you may not be able to respond to.

Name: _____ **Today's date:** _____

This questionnaire describes problems and complaints that people sometimes have. Please read it carefully. After you have done so, please tick the appropriate box which best describes how you have felt in the past week, including today. Tick only one column for each of the problems listed.

		0	1	2	3
		NOT A PROBLEM ZERO TIMES A WEEK	**LITTLE PROBLEM** ONCE A WEEK	**MODERATE PROBLEM** SEVERAL TIMES A WEEK	**MARKED PROBLEM** AT LEAST ONCE A DAY
1	Am preoccupied with one or two things				
2	Feeling depressed or low				
3	Others have difficulty following what I am saying				
4	I have difficulty concentrating				
5	Feeling as if my thoughts might not be my own				
6	Feeling as if I am being watched				
7	Feeling useless or helpless				
8	Feeling confused or puzzled				
9	Feeling stubborn or refusing to carry out simple requests				
10	Feeling very excited				
11	Feeling forgetful or 'far away'				
12	Being open and explicit about sexual matters				
13	My speech comes out jumbled or is full of odd words				
14	Sleep has been restless or unsettled				
15	Behaving oddly for no reason				
16	Feeling unable to cope, having difficulty managing everyday tasks and interest				

   P

		0	1	2	3
		NOT A PROBLEM ZERO TIMES A WEEK	LITTLE PROBLEM ONCE A WEEK	MODERATE PROBLEM SEVERAL TIMES A WEEK	MARKED PROBLEM AT LEAST ONCE A DAY
17	Not feeling like eating				
18	Feeling like playing tricks or pranks				
19	Feeling quiet or withdrawn				
20	Talking or smiling to myself				
21	Not bothered about appearance or hygiene				
22	Feeling violent				
23	Thinking I could be someone else				
24	Feeling dissatisfied with myself				
25	Having aches and pains				
26	Losing my temper easily				
27	Having no interest in things				
28	Feeling as if I am being laughed at or talked about				
29	Feeling tired or lacking in energy				
30	Movements seem slow				
31	Feeling as if my thoughts might be controlled				
32	Feeling aggressive or pushy				
33	Feeling irritable or quick tempered				
34	Feeling tense, afraid or anxious				
TOTAL SCORE					

Used with permission of authors, **Dr Jo Smith** and **Professor Max Birchwood.** Reference **Birchwood, M et al** (1989) 'Predicting Relapse in Schizophrenia', *Psychological Medicine*, 19, 649–56.

Problem solving

It helps if relatives are aware of the part played by stress in schizophrenia and of the vicious circle of pressure from relatives, or the environment, that can lead to exacerbation of symptoms or problems. This vicious circle can be broken at several points, one of which is to develop a system for solving problems. There are always going to be problems, and although you can get useful advice from professionals, it is important that the family becomes good at solving these problems. Learning the skills to solve problems is a first step in dealing with all the specific difficulties a family will have.

The six stages of problem solving

❶ **Identify a specific problem:** this means defining the problem clearly, avoiding woolly terms. Avoid words like 'lazy' or 'difficult' and state clearly exactly what the problem is (eg, 'John stays in bed until midday and this upsets mum').

❷ **List alternative solutions:** sit down with your family and discuss as many alternatives as possible, for example. 'Let him stay in bed and don't worry', 'Buy him an alarm clock', 'Let him lie in late three mornings a week', 'Give him something to get up for'.

❸ **Discuss pros and cons:** What are the effects of letting John lie in bed? How does it make us feel? Is it our problem? Does it do him any damage? Find out why it upsets mum, does she believe he could be employed if he were not in bed?

❹ **Choose the best solution:** A compromise. John can stay in bed on Saturday and Sunday, but on certain days he will get up by ten o'clock. We will build into his day something to get up for eg, a trip out.

❺ **Plan how to implement the solution:** Sally gives him a call and takes him a cup of tea rather than dad shouting at him. We'll make a written contract including John, if we all agree, and we'll sign it. Then we'll meet in two weeks and discuss it.

❻ **Review efforts:** Look at how things have developed. What are the obstacles? Expect problems and don't be surprised when they occur.

P

What is the Mental Health Act?

The Act is the legal framework to ensure that proper care is provided for people with mental disorders. Legislation has radically changed since it first appeared in 1845, when mentally ill people had to be 'certified' by a local magistrate before admission to hospital. The spirit of the act is that treatment or care on a compulsory basis is very much a last resort, and voluntary treatment is always preferred if consent can be obtained. Where necessary, the Act does provide for compulsory admission, detention and treatment. This usually only applies if the health and safety of the patient is in question, or to protect others.

How long can a person be kept in?

If a person with a severe mental disorder refuses to enter hospital on the recommendation of a doctor, then on the application of the nearest relative, or an approved social worker, the person can be admitted compulsorily for varying lengths of time. This is known as being 'admitted under section'. The most frequently used sections are the following: **Section 4:** Up to 72 hours in an emergency for assessment; **Section 2:** Up to 28 days for assessment and treatment (patients can appeal to the Mental Health Review Tribunal within 14 days of being admitted); **Section 3:** Up to six months for treatment (again, patients can appeal to the MHRT); **Section 136:** Up to 72 hours; a police officer can take a person from a public place, if suffering from a severe mental disorder to a 'place of safety', usually a hospital.

Can the family get their relative admitted?

If the family feels that their relative needs to be admitted under compulsory powers, they should ask their GP for advice, or contact the local social services department, who will send a social worker to look into the situation.

Can a doctor treat patients without their consent?

Medication can be given for three months, without patients' consent, if they are kept in hospital under Section 2 (28 days) or Section 3 (six months). After three months, it may be given if the person agrees to it. If the person does not consent, medication can be given if a second doctor from the Mental Health Act Commission also approves of the treatment.

Can a nurse stop patients leaving?

Nurses may detain a patient for up to six hours, either for that person's health and safety, or to protect others. This is to allow time for a doctor to arrive and to decide if the person should be kept in hospital or be allowed to leave.

Does the hospital have to help the patient after leaving hospital?

Health and social services must provide after-care services for people who have been kept in hospital for six months or longer until it is felt that it is no longer needed.

What do you do if you have any complaints?

A committee has been set up called the Mental Health Act Commission to make sure that legislation is applied properly. The Commission consists of 90 professionals from the fields of medicine, law, psychology and social work, as well as lay members. They visit hospitals regularly and the medical members give second opinions.

❶ Alzheimer's disease is a physical illness which causes a progressive decline in the ability to remember, to learn, to think and to reason. It was first described by a German neurologist, Alois Alzheimer, in 1907. It is the most common form of dementia, accounting for 50 per cent of those diagnosed as having dementia. Another 20 per cent have multi-infarct dementia and another 20 per cent have both. Ten per cent have a variety of rarer forms of dementia.

The loss of short-term memory is the most striking early sign. As the disease progresses, the loss of the ability to think, reason and grasp complex ideas becomes more and more marked. Simple tasks like trying shoelaces or telling the time become difficult. As the disease takes hold, sufferers become increasingly less aware of their condition.

❷ The disease is associated with changes in the neurons in the outer layer of the brain which cause the brain to shrink. Under a microscope it is possible to see damaged brain cells forming 'tangles' and 'plaques'. There are also biochemical changes, with a noticeable reduction in the neurotransmitter acetylcholine. The cause of Alzheimer's disease is unknown, but it is known that it is not caused by hardening of the arteries, under or overuse of the brain, or the effects of stress. There is some evidence that there is excess aluminium found in the brains of people with Alzheimer's. This does not mean that the disease is caused simply by exposure to aluminium. It affects all sections of society, and both sexes equally. There is no known curative treatment.

❸ Prevalence of dementia in the population is:

Ages 40–65	less than 1 per cent
Ages 65–70	2 per cent
Ages 70–80	5 per cent
Ages 80 and above	20 per cent

There is some evidence of a genetic influence with a slight but definite familial tendency. This is a stronger genetic link where age of onset is relatively low (between 35 and 60 years).

❹ The onset of Alzheimers is gradual and frequently comes to the attention as a result of some acute disturbance such as an illness, a change of environment or a bereavement. Usually diagnosis occurs a while after the onset of the illness. Decline can be rapid in some people, gradual or uneven in others. Some people can live up to 20 years, but most live for 6–12 years after onset.

❺ Dementia does not only affect the patient. It profoundly changes the lives of all family members and friends involved. Help from health and social workers is geared towards reducing the stress and strain on caring relatives, as well as alleviating as many unpleasant consequences of the condition as possible.

P

Multi-infarct dementia

This form of dementia accounts for 20 per cent of all dementias and is the result of death of brain tissue (infarction) after a series of very small strokes or 'strokelets'. Brain cells in a small area of the brain are killed, either because the blood supply to that area is blocked (thrombo-embolic infarction), or because the blood vessels burst (haemorrhagic infarction), releasing blood into that area of the brain. Each stroke may be so small that the sufferer doesn't actually notice.

Persistant high blood pressure is one factor which has been identified as causing damage to the walls of small blood vessels in the brain. Typically the illness progresses in a stepwise fashion in which mental function deteriorates and then stabilises. Special features of multi-infarct dementia include a greater degree of awareness and insight.

Pick's disease

Pick's disease is a rare degenerative disease which particularly affects the front of the person's brain, leading to loss of judgement and disinhibition. It is most common in women and usually begins between the ages of 50 and 60 years. Early symptoms tend to be changes in behaviour and personality. So far the cause for the disease is unknown and no specific treatment exists.

Huntington's disease (Huntington's Chorea)

This disease affects approximately 3,000 people in the United Kingdom at any one time. It is an inherited degenerative disease, due to a dominant gene, which means that one half of all offspring can be expected to develop the disease. Huntington's Chorea specifically affects the motor control system, and so early symptoms include twitching of limbs or muscles in the face. There is no specific cure but certain drugs can reduce irregular movement to some degree.

Parkinson's disease

Parkinson's disease is due to a loss of nerve cells and the neurotransmitter dopamine, which they contain. Characteristic symptoms, which often arise gradually, are tremor, stillness of limbs, and slowness of movement, speech and thought. Drug treatments which modify dopamine levels can cause improvement in the movement disorder.

HIV/AIDS dementia

Dementia is common in the later stages of the HIV/AIDS illness, although subtle mild symptoms such as impaired attention and impaired fine motor speed may be observed early on.

Cruetzfeldt-Jacob disease

This is a very rare dementing illness that runs a very rapid cause. On average there are 30 new cases a year in the UK. Most patients die within 2 years. Florid psychiatric symptoms such as delusions and hallucinations are often seen. The illness is transmissible, but the precise agent of transmission remains unknown.

Lewy Body disease

Lewy Body disease is characterised by fluctuating impairment in memory and cognitive skills, and visual and auditory hallucination. It is often mistaken for schizophrenia.

Semantic dementia

This is a form of dementia that starts off with very pronounced language impairment. The sufferer often cannot find the right words to identify things and their ability to comprehend language is impaired. Often there is evidence of an acquired dyslexia in reading and spelling skills. Memory, perceptual skills and non verbal problem solving are initially well preserved.

Other Dementias

There is no fixed pattern of symptoms and no fixed speed of deterioration. People react differently but what is certain is that they will get worse. The following stages give a rough guide to the course of the illness.

◼ Mild dementia

◆ Apathy: less interested in hobbies, activities and new things.

◆ More forgetful of details of recent events. More likely to repeat self and lose the thread of conversation. Routine, over-learned tasks are performed adequately.

◆ Less good at making decisions, planning and grasping complex ideas.

◆ More self-centred and less concerned for others and their feelings.

◆ More irritable and upset if they fail at something.

◼ Moderate dementia

◆ Being very forgetful of recent events. Forgetting names of friends and relatives. Leaving saucepans and kettles to boil over. Being more repetitive. Memory for past events is usually good.

◆ Confusion over time and place – may wander off and get lost. Rapidly becoming lost if in unfamiliar surroundings.

◆ Being more clinging and emotional. Becoming angry, upset or distressed rapidly.

◆ Misunderstanding and misinterpreting situations eg, 'You are abandoning me', or 'they are stealing from me'. Occasionally hearing or seeing things that are not there.

◆ Being neglectful of hygiene or eating, saying that they have had a bath or a meal when they haven't.

◆ Less fluent in everyday conversation – word finding difficulties.

◼ Severe dementia

◆ Memory is very poor, usually unable to remember for even a few minutes. Forget that they have just had a meal. Unable to find their way around. Shows poor recognition of friends or relatives.

◆ Often repeating one phrase or sound.

◆ Sometimes incontinent of urine and/or faeces.

◆ Needing help and supervision with feeding, washing, bathing, dressing and using the toilet.

◆ Being restless and sometimes aggressive, especially when feeling threatened or closed in.

P

■ Be adaptable – allow for changes

Understand and accept the nature of the illness. You and the sufferer are trying to make the best of a bad situation – accept that change is a necessity. If the sufferer can eat more successfully with a spoon, but finds it difficult to manage a knife and fork, accept the change; don't fight it. Try to maintain a sense of humour.

■ Try to create the right environment

Confused people with poor memories need a familiar, established structured environment that is constant, predictable and simple. Try to build regular events into the weekly timetable. A calm, relaxed, unpressurised atmosphere will help draw out the best of their abilities. Provide memory aids such as a large calendar, clocks, a reminder board, signposts and labels and a large diary.

■ Encourage as much independence as possible

The longer sufferers are able to do things for themselves the longer they will be able to maintain a sense of dignity and self-worth, and avoid feelings of helplessness. It is very important to keep a balance between encouraging them to do things for themselves and doing things for them. Don't expect them to do everything, but don't take over. The attitude should be, 'Let me help you with that', rather than, 'Let me do it for you'. It is also important to offer protection from situations where they might fail, so instead of saying, 'You can cook the meal tonight' say, 'Could you help me peel the potatoes tonight'.

■ Keep communicating

When sufferers are confused, have a poor memory, and are emotionally upset, their most important fundamental need is to be able to communicate. Starved of communication with the outside world we all suffer. Two-way communication with a sufferer of dementia is a difficult, challenging, but ultimately rewarding task. Take into account and compensate for their sensory deficits. Is one ear better than the other? Are they short-sighted? Speak clearly, slowly and in short simple sentences. Allow them longer to respond – be prepared to repeat yourself if necessary. Talk about the past, using photographs and mementos to aid recall. Reminiscence is a valuable way of facilitating communication, as it is enjoyable and helps the person feel they are giving something back. Use touch to keep attention. Most importantly, be prepared to try to interpret and make sense of the meaning behind the sufferer's often confused words and thoughts. Recognise feelings from body language and facial expression.

■ Look after yourself

It is very common for carers to neglect themselves. Find time for a break and continue to do the things that you enjoy. Look for as much social support as possible. Encourage friends and relatives to become involved. If there are financial and legal arrangements to be made contact the Citizens Advice Bureau in the UK.

Looking after a loved one who is gradually disintegrating as a person, while one's lifestyle is becoming increasingly restricted, isolated and exhausting, triggers a whole range of emotions in the carer. It is helpful to acknowledge that these emotions are perfectly normal.

■ Grief

As the patient's illness progresses, you may experience the loss of a companion, the loss of an important relationship and the loss of how things were. In one sense it is like a loved one having died, but in another sense they are still there. Just when you think you have adjusted, you may find the patient has changed and you go through the grieving experience again. Allow these feelings to come out; try not to bottle them up. It *is* very sad.

■ Guilt

It is common to feel guilty at losing your temper with the sufferer, to feel guilty about being embarrassed at their odd behaviour, guilty for not wanting the responsibility, guilty for placing them in a home or in hospital and for feeling relief when they are not there. It is important to recognise those feelings so that you can make clear-minded decisions about the future, and do what is best for the whole family. Don't expect yourself to be perfect!

■ Anger and aggression

It is natural to feel angry and frustrated: angry that it has happened to you; angry that others don't seem to be helping out; angry at the sufferer for his or her difficult behaviour; angry at inadequate services; angry at the role-reversal that may have taken place. It is helpful to share you feeling with others. It is also useful to recognise an increase in these feelings as a signal that you need a break or more help. Also it is helpful to try to distinguish between being angry at the sufferer's behaviour and being angry at the person. Dementia sufferers are ill and can't help their behaviour. Remember that this difficult behaviour is not aimed at you personally.

■ Embarrassment

It is easy to get embarrassed if your relative is screaming and shouting. Perhaps the walls are thin and you find yourself thinking, 'I don't know what the neighbours will be thinking'. It helps to explain the illness to them, as most people are quite ignorant of the effect of Alzheimer's disease. Real friends will be able to overcome the embarrassment caused by the sufferer's poor table manners, sloppiness or repetition.

■ Mixed feelings

The majority of carers experience a mixture of negative and positive feelings. The positive feelings are based on the strength of the previous relationship and the satisfaction of caring for a loved one. Intense mixed feelings indicate a relationship that really matters. Bottling up mixed feelings does not help. On the other hand, expressing negative feelings in an uncontrolled outburst is not always helpful. The best ways is perhaps the middle road of expressing feelings in a safe way by talking to a good friend or confidant, or somebody else in a similar position.

P

It is very common for people with dementia, or any other brain injury, to behave in an aggressive manner. This may take the form of verbal abuse, damage to property, or physical violence. It is important to avoid interpreting this behaviour as if it came from a healthy person.

The greatest aggression is often directed at the closest relatives. This is because you are there and are perhaps a safer target. It is not personal or calculated. Do not fall into the trap of reading anything further into this aggression, such as that they are getting their own back on you, or that they hate you.

The best way of coping is firstly to identify potential triggers; secondly to identify preventative measures; thirdly to identify ways of coping; and fourthly to identify ways of coping with yourself afterwards.

Common triggers

◆ Feeling humiliated if forced to accept help with intimate functions.

◆ Feeling a failure for not coping.

◆ Feeling pressurised.

◆ Misunderstanding events, for example accusing people of stealing when the patient has mislaid something.

◆ Fear – no longer recognising people.

◆ Boredom, having excess energy.

◆ Feeling ill or in pain.

Preventative measures

◆ Create a calm, stress-free environment in which the patient does not feel confused or rushed.

◆ Explain what is happening – give a running commentary.

◆ Encourage independence – offer help but don't take over.

◆ Avoid confrontation by distracting attention.

◆ Praise achievement and avoid criticism.

◆ Make sure the sufferer has plenty of exercise and interest.

◆ Try to avoid direct requests such as 'Don't do that', or 'Get dressed now'.

Coping with aggression

◆ React calmly, don't argue or raise your voice, try to show no fear, count to ten (or 20).

◆ Do not take personal offence, it is part of the illness.

◆ Do not use punishment.

◆ Allow the sufferer plenty of personal space – do not get too close or cornered, or attempt to lead them away.

◆ Defuse the situation by distraction and providing alternative activities.

◆ Bear in mind forgetfulness is an advantage, they are likely to quickly forget the episode.

Coping with yourself

◆ Try to remain detached – do not be provoked.

◆ Do not feel guilty if you are provoked – you are under great stress.

◆ Do not bottle it up – go and talk to somebody.

◆ Try not to take it personally, you may get the brunt of the aggression because you are a safe target.

Wandering

Wandering is a common and stressful problem for carers of relatives with dementia. Not only are you like to feel concerned for their safety but you may also feel guilty that they have managed to slip away. But nobody can be expected to keep a 24-hour watch on somebody else, so some degree of risk is inevitable.

Wandering can occur for a variety of reasons, such as loss of short-term memory resulting in confusion; feeling uncertain and disorientated in a new environment; as a way of using up excess energy, and an outlet for expressing boredom; or searching for something or someone related to the past.

When you find your relative he or she is likely to be confused and frightened. Try not to scold or show your anxiety. Reassure the patient and return to a familiar routine as quickly as possible.

Avoid giving your relative medication to prevent wandering. Doses which are powerful enough to achieve this have unfortunate side-effects, such as drowsiness, which often increases confusion and incontinence.

Make sure your relative carries some form of identification in case of getting lost, for example, an identity bracelet with name and telephone number. It makes sense to tell neighbours and local shopkeepers about the problem. Most people are helpful once they understand the situation.

Sometimes it may help to put a lock or bolt on the door that sufferers are not familiar with. If they are determined to leave the house it is best not to confront them too severely, but rather try following them a little way, and then divert their attention so that you can return home together.

Incontinence

The first step when dealing with any problem of incontinence, whether it be urinary, faecal, or constipation, is to consult your GP. The problem may be caused by a medical condition such as a urinary tract infection, or by the side-effects of medication.

An important initial intervention involves keeping a record or a diary sheet for a week or so, to monitor how often the person is wet, when it occurs, and how often they go to the toilet. Try to identify a pattern or any situations which tend to precipitate incontinence.

You may be able to avoid many accidents by taking your relative to the lavatory at regular intervals. Also, become more alert to the tell-tale signs that your relative wants to go, such as fidgeting or pulling at their clothes. Clothes which are easy to remove or unfasten are an advantage, for example, tracksuit trousers.

Make sure that the lavatory is easy to reach and is comfortable. If it is a distance to the lavatory, a commode loaned from social services or the health authority may be useful.

If incontinence occurs at night, try cutting down on fluids several hours before bedtime but make sure your relative drinks plenty of fluids for the rest of the day. Make sure that they use the lavatory before going to bed.

If incontinence cannot be controlled through regular toileting, it may make sense for your relative to wear incontinence pads or underwear during the day.

Try to get over your embarrassment – be tactful and sensitive. Sometimes a little humour is useful for relieving the tension. Finally, remember that although the situation is difficult for you, it is also humiliating for your relative. Try to remain calm and matter-of-fact; remember it is not the patient's fault.

P

Subject Index

P